The Essence
of Self-Healing

The
Essence
of
Self-Healing

How to bring health and
happiness into your life

Petrene Soames

Fleet Street
PUBLICATIONS

© 2000 Petrene Soames. All right reserved.
First printed March 2001

FleetStreet Publications
Box 130416
Spring, TX 77393-0416 USA

Book cover and interior design by Lightbourne
Back cover photograph by Arthur Garcia
Printed in the United States of America

Publisher's Cataloging-in-Publication
(Provided by Quality Books, Inc.)
Soames, Petrene
    The essence of self-healing: how to bring
health and happiness into your life / Petrene
Soames -- 1st ed.
    p. cm.
    Includes index.
    LCCN: 00-104317
    ISBN: 0-9700444-0-2

    1. Mental healing. 2. Psychic ability.
I. Title.

    RZ400.S63 2001   615.8'52
                QBI00-477

All personal vignettes and stories are true. Identifying information has been altered.

"The swiftest thing to fly is the mind.
Those who know this have wings."

–The Hopi

Acknowledgements

༈

My love and thanks to Etal for his total dedication and for helping my message become more understandable.

Many thanks to Jane Marie Heid for her tireless research and help in a hundred different ways.

Thanks to everyone who helped make this book a reality.

Last, but not least, thank you, the reader, for opening your heart and mind to "The Essence of Self-Healing."

About the Author

～

Petrene Soames is a leading authority in healing and self-awareness. For more than 20 years she has worked successfully in the field of wellness and in helping others achieve their personal potential. Her unique practices and insights, which are drawn from every realm of human sciences and studies, have helped hundred of clients worldwide.

Petrene has been called a therapist, a healer, a consultant, a medium, and a world-class psychic. Whatever the terminology, as a therapist Petrene works without the use of hypnosis and delves into the realms of Rebirthing (*a powerful experience which releases past emotional blocks, pains, traumas, fears and angers*), Regression (*present and past life therapy*), Progression (*forward time and life experience*), and Digression (*parallel realities*).

Over the past 10 years, Petrene has been more focused on healing and healthcare, further developing her techniques. She has been working with children and adults covering a wide range of diseases and illnesses, from headaches and allergies to heart disease and cancer.

"Your healing sessions have changed my life—more specifically, you have allowed me the opportunity to embrace who I truly am. Furthermore, you have provided an incredible source of true transformation to awaken me to the full capacity of my essence!"
—Shawnda Hibbeler, Montgomery, Texas

As a motivating and inspirational speaker, Petrene's goal

is to help people take control of their lives and their health, giving them the opportunity to discover the person that they truly are. Her message is clear and simple: "I am amazing, and you are amazing, too! If you don't truly know this, it's time to believe in yourself and let the magic be." As a veteran radio and television talk show guest both here and in England, Petrene has dazzled audiences with her incredible powers. (She is the first and only psychic to transport two people to the future live on national TV in Europe!)

Petrene realizes that most people don't have a good understanding of what a genuine psychic is or does. She emphasizes that people should not confuse her work with that of "readers," or those who can be found on the "Psychic Hot Line," or now the Internet "Psychics." As a clairvoyant, one who sees clearly, Petrene works without mediums such as cards, crystal balls, etc. She is a genuine psychic who works with ESP, needing only a vibration to tune into, such as a name, a voice, a photograph, or a piece of handwriting. She is in a class all of her own beyond New Age and other concepts.

Her work is devoted to the individual, bringing deeper awareness by cutting through perceptions and conceptions, and stepping out and beyond the limited reality that we all perceive ourselves to be in. Her amazing abilities bring a new meaning to the term "psychic."

Petrene has appeared on numerous television and radio programs both in England and throughout the United States, and has been featured in national and international newspapers and magazines. She even wrote a monthly column for a North London newspaper for several years. "In Europe, healers and psychics are much more accepted and respected," says Petrene. "In America, the public have been burned, but there is plenty of room here for positive change."

In *The Essence of Self-Healing*, Petrene brings to a wider audience her groundbreaking work in wellness, offering everyone the tools they need to heal and feel great. The book is unique in its simplicity, and clarity. It reminds all of us of our own self-healing skills. Written with warmth, charm and profound insights, it delivers a refreshing, invigorating, and empowering feeling. It focuses on building a better understanding of the links between our thoughts, our beliefs, and our health. It gives step-by-step instructions, easy-to use techniques and exercises that can be simply adjusted to individual needs. Packed with practical information, tips and true stories of people who have healed themselves, it is an invaluable resource for everyone in need of renewed health and happiness. Healing works and can help with anything from a headache to serious illnesses. Petrene stresses that her techniques are not meant as a replacement for traditional medicine, but are certainly a powerful complement.

Originally from England, and widely traveled, Petrene now lives in The Woodlands, Texas (Houston area), where she continues her fascinating work.

"Psychics, love'em or hate'em, believe or disbelieve, there's no denying that everyone is fascinated by these mystic gurus. And after you've met Petrene, you may even be convinced about their powers...."
—Andrew Balkin, London Regional Newspapers

Contents

༅

Chapter 1

Why Self-Healing?

✦

Introduction

Although many books have been written on self-healing, very few seem to work for everyone. In many of these books, the terms used, the answers given, and the exercises recommended often complicate the subject, and bring or reinforce theories and concepts that are not necessarily so. Now is the time to address the ridiculousness of the present health-care situation, especially in the United States, where endless amounts of drugs, drug alternatives and natural solutions are widely available and constantly advertised, yet still millions of people continue to be in poor health. Health issues have become very complex, and yet we will see throughout this book that self-healing is simple. Two reasons clearly stand out as to why we do not heal: a lack of self-belief and a lack of knowledge.

I have been working as a healer, intuitive, therapist and counselor in the healing and self-awareness fields for over twenty years. During this time, I have met thousands of individuals who were not well and were out of balance, and I have realized that illness is a choice, although it may not initially appear that way. This is a basic fact. There are countless reasons why people make the choice to be or to remain ill. Throughout this book, we will examine those choices, and we will see how we can learn to use our power wisely by choosing to be well, without the use of outside products. Personally, I am rarely ill. When I do get ill, it is with very minor problems. It is simply not in my reality to be ill, not because I am "lucky" or have "strong genes," but because I do not choose illness for myself. I have successfully used self-healing for as long as I can remember. In chapter 9 I will share some simple exercises that I use, and that others have used, whenever there is a need to get back in balance. I have had the opportunity to meet many people who also have successfully healed themselves treating a wide range of problems and ailments.

The true stories presented in chapter 10 are examples of people just like you and I who have healed themselves, some of them after many years of being in pain and having visited numerous professionals without success. I hope that their stories will inspire you in your own self-healing journey.

Finally, I decided to write *The Essence of Self-Healing* because I have seen over and over that self-healing works. I believe that it is time for a far greater number of people to have access to another point of view, a simpler one, that may further inspire them to look more deeply into themselves, and regain once again the realization and the belief of how truly amazing we really all are.

A time and place for healing

Time and time again we have observed the body's own healing mechanisms. For example, when we cut ourselves or suffer insect bites, our body heals with little or no outside help. We also hear many stories of people who have recovered from "incurable" diseases against all odds. Without a doubt, our body has its own self-healing mechanisms. We may have been told this in a vague and abstract way, but few of us have explored this truth in depth. Although there are people who successfully use self-healing, at the present time they are a minority. Two simple reasons illustrate why this is so. First, as individuals, we have been subjected to conditioning that makes us doubt the fact that we can heal ourselves. We are often discouraged by the belief that self-healing is a difficult or complex process or that strict regimes must be followed to ensure success. Second, although we might suspect that we all have the inner knowledge of how to heal ourselves, we may still believe that it is beyond our comprehension to access this knowledge, imagining we must undertake a journey of many long years in self-study. So instead, most of us stay ruled by our own fear, shame and pain.

Self-healing is not a major part of our world because we give it little space and accept many different concepts, percepts and beliefs instead. In order to accept healing, wholeness and perfect health, we will need to recognize our responsibility for the presence of imbalance within our lives and ourselves.

Challenging our thinking

Much of our reality has been created and endorsed by philosophers hundred of years ago. We look upon them as "great thinkers," never presuming that we have the mental capacity to go beyond their established thinking. We learn belief systems, theories and facts and are rarely invited to challenge them. Few of us ever do. It is understandable that, with our conditioning and acceptance of what we have been taught, only a few people truly open their minds, explore their own awareness, and discover realities beyond the limitations of what has previously been thought. Often people tend to accept that "there is nothing new under the sun." This is not necessarily true, and can be viewed as a mental block that prevents us from seeing beyond it. It's important, as we will see later, that during the self-healing process we recognize these blocks in our thoughts, beliefs and creativity.

Words can also act as blocks when we accept them without feeling and thinking what they mean to us personally. In this book, I will use the words "consciousness" and "awareness" to convey a much bigger reality both within and outside of ourselves. But it is important to ask yourself what these words mean to you, because many times we accept words and concepts without thinking and feeling what they mean and bring to us, as individuals. We do not need to go along with what everyone else thinks or assumes. But we truly need to find truth for ourselves. Remember the story of the Emperor and his new clothes? It goes something like this: Once there was an Emperor who ordered a tailor to make him a beautiful, expensive suit of clothes. Instead, the tailor took the money and the cloth for himself and only pretended to put new clothes on the Emperor. Then he stood back, looked at the Emperor standing naked and assured the great man he looked wonderful, telling him that only a fool would not be able to see his fine clothes, the richness of the cloth and the perfect fit of the garments. The Emperor's courtiers were horrified to see the great man with no clothes on. But as the word went around, they heard that only a fool would not be able to see the fine new suit of clothes. One by one, they fawned and admired and assured the Emperor he looked magnificent and that a finer suit of clothes could never be found. This went on day after day until one day a small boy in the street broke out laughing and shouted, "He's got no clothes on!" The little boy did not know or care if he looked like a fool. He spoke the truth and reality as he saw it. The spell of false reality had been broken.

Many of us go along with words like "soul," "spirit," "imagination," "awareness" and "consciousness," or concepts of "guides," "guardian angels" and such things, without ever having a complete understanding of what these words mean to us. Try asking other people what they think these words and concepts mean. You will probably get many different answers. By all means, take their opinions into account, but above all, ask yourself: what do these words mean to me? Through the true and real answers that you have within yourself, you can open the doorway to your own limitless realizations and realities. After all, there are no real experts on what is real and what is not, only a billion different opinions. And yours is as valid as everyone else's.

As we move into the third millennium, our thinking will be challenged again and again when we see that great seers and prophets from the past have predicted much that does not actually take place. The world does not end after all. Who can we begin to believe then? We will have to turn inward and begin to believe in ourselves and discover all of which we actually are. We can then begin to realize that suffering is not our only path or duty. It's more like a record that has been played over and over. But there are other tunes to play.

"Being" brings to mind a concept popular in the sixties; it conjures up visions of cross-legged gurus, lotus blossoms and a utopian style of existence. But "Being" also suggests quietness and stillness. "Being" can be a positive concept. So can "doing." There is no right or wrong way here, only two different paths among many others, different ways of thinking and relating to reality and to what reality brings and means to us. Reading something many times, or listening to many people's similar views of reality, does not make these views real or final. We need to accept that we have preferences, as do others.

Venturing beyond our present time and our present beliefs about who we are, we still have much to discover about ourselves. Teachers and helpers along the way can and will be found, not only from the outside, but also within ourselves.

Time appears to be moving very fast, often at almost

breakneck speed. We marvel at the breakthroughs in modern technology and yet, the changes to make our lives easier and stress free, seem small. Much discovered is not available and many individuals do not feel that they have the time that they need to find and be with themselves. The answer is loud and clear. If you don't have time, make time. Remember, however unreal it seems, time is yours. It may well be all that you have.

When we view our world as it now appears, we can travel the depressive, but also realistic, route. Millions of people still exist in poverty, even in affluent societies. Over twelve million children in the United States go hungry, and many of them are homeless. Ignorance and violence thrive as does war, which it would seem is a vast source of entertainment on television.

But we can also choose to look from another perspective. So much is changing every day. The most wonderful things are happening. Advances are being made. Illumination and love is thriving in even the darkest of places. Communication has expanded. Subjects that were once taboo are now being more openly discussed. Millions of people want positive change and are prepared to work to that end for themselves and for future generations.

We need to seriously ask ourselves now: Do we want positive change in our lives, to be happy and whole, to love and be loved, and to experience joy? Do we want to experience the fulfillment of our potential? Are we ready to heal? There are always elements both in us and outside of us that would have us believe we cannot heal and are not in charge. We hear from psychologists that most people only use 10 percent of their brain, as if this somehow makes everything all right. By the way, who said that consciousness, and the knowledge of who we are, has anything to do with the brain anyway? This is another example of a widely accepted concept that has never been proved and may not even be true.

What is illness and imbalance?

I have said that illness and imbalance are a conscious choice, and that there are many different reasons for making that choice. This may be very difficult to accept if you have a loved one who is dying of cancer. But as you stay longer with the process of unraveling the mind and the emotions, you will see that it is so. Imbalance can be a desired way of being and as useful to us as balance. It is our choice to decide how long a state of imbalance lasts. We have the answers and the knowledge within us to restore balance to an imbalanced state of being.

To say that illness is the result of imbalance is a quick answer to a very complex, and yet at the same time simple, subject. But with thought, it is a subject that can be unraveled, realized and changed within us all. We will need to go further into ourselves, beyond anything written or thought, before we can discover that, after all, there are no imperfections, only differences. But we have become biased towards the view of imperfection being bad, rooted deeply in our minds within concepts that have truly never been our own. Look at the popular singer Rod Stewart. He has a deep gravel voice, which may be considered imperfect by many. And yet, the artist used his voice to produce records loved by millions. Helen Keller's blindness might have been considered also as imperfection. However, she developed her personality and communication skills in ways unknown, before becoming a legend and inspiration during and far beyond her own lifetime. She was certainly the first deaf-blind person to make such a public success of her life. After her death in 1968 an organization was set up in her name to combat blindness in the developing world. When we look at the idiosyncrasy of past and present geniuses, all peculiarities appear to be forgiven and understood when viewed in the light of their often spectacular offerings to mankind.

In our present, and in many ways exciting times, differences are being explored and integrated, even held up for our inspection and understanding. Differences and imperfections are no longer now so often ignored, but rather valued, and slowly integrated into that great and colorful mass of matter which contains thoughts, emotions and experiences, and that each one of us, as individuals, lends ourselves to, making up together the wonderful thing which we call humanity and reality.

Back to simplicity

Simplicity is a valuable tool in our self-healing process. Modern medicine and science might lead us to believe that the healing process is highly complex. There may be truth in this also, but we can focus on simplicity and have it work for us. It is wonderful to expand your vision and your awareness to watch the healing process taking place. It is wonderful to realize the simplicity, as well as the complexity of the emotions, times and events, which led you to your initial choice of illness and imbalance. For, as you look closer, and become more aware, you will see the interconnectedness of everything. During your self-healing work, keep things simple, because they are. Choosing the path of simplicity does not mean that you label yourself, or will be labeled, as naïve. On the contrary, it means that you are aware enough, and trusting enough of yourself, to realize that simplicity is an important and very real pathway to follow.

Simplicity will work time and time again where complexity often fails. For example, if you ask yourself: "Why do I have a pain in my shoulder or cramps in my legs?" and you feel and receive the answer, "Because I do not feel loved and cared for, I am not receiving enough attention from those I love," accept this answer, as it may well be as simple as that. This answer may also be true for far greater and more complex illnesses and imbalances. Work with the simple answers you receive and follow through with your own simple actions. There is no need to look for problems when they often do not exist, although it is easy to slip into complex self-diagnosis as well as seek outside diagnosis and theories. At the same time, do not allow yourself to become over anxious about aches and pains, or even bigger problems, when you know you are already dealing with them. We will explore in this book the concept of tough and easy ways of doing things, and we will see why we often choose the hard ways. For now, it is important to remember that we have a choice. During your experiences with self-healing, you may hear a little voice in your head saying: "It cannot be that simple!" But the truth is: Yes it can!

Why do we need self-healing? The facts.

We are without a doubt in a time of change. Of course, this has always been true, but we appear to be more focused and aware of change now. Our own health and related issues are more talked about, more written about and researched by more people than ever before. Health has also become a vast enterprise in a growing market. Just look at how many times a week you receive brochures and supplements through the mail, even to the point of free painkillers. Recently, an article published in Ladies' Home Journal (April 1999) stated that the pharmaceutical industry spent over one billion dollars on its advertising campaign each year.

Despite the efforts, the facts are that in the United States, the three leading causes of death have remained virtually unchanged. According to a report in 1998 conducted by the National Center for the Health Statistics, heart disease caused an estimated 725,790 deaths in 1997, compared with 733,361 deaths in 1996; cancer caused 537,390 deaths in 1997 and 539,533 the year before; and strokes caused 159,877 deaths in 1998, and 159,942 in 1996. Rounding out the top ten killer diseases are chronic lung disease, accidents, pneumonia and influenza, diabetes, suicide, kidney diseases and bacterial blood infections. Incidentally, the death rate from AIDS is now on the decline. It is now no longer in the top ten but rates fourteenth compared to eighth in 1996.

In spite of the sizable fortune spent on medicine in the United States, very little money is spent to treat the causes of chronic diseases before major illnesses develop. The Centers for Disease Control reports that 54 percent of heart disease, 37 percent of cancer, 50 percent of cerebrovascular disease (strokes) and 49 percent of arteriosclerosis (hardening of the arteries) is preventable through lifestyle modification. Some drugs also seem to lose their efficacy. Within the past few years, numerous articles have been written on the inability of penicillin and other antibiotics to fight the increasing variety of viruses. Numerous statistics have been quoted from medical journals and sources stating that because antibiotics have been over prescribed there is now a growing resistance to them by many viruses. In an article titled "Antibiotics losing their fight: evolving bacteria prove too much for drugs" published by ABC News in December 1998, Lauran Neergarrd points out that "doctors once predicted that antibiotics would vanquish infectious diseases. But germs instead are increasingly evolving ways to overpower antibiotics, a danger fast reaching crisis proportions."

There is another problem associated with the use of prescription drugs. The number of elderly people is rising. At the turn of this century, there will be more older people living than children. On September 9, 1999, Reuters Health stated, that in a report published in the September issue of Psychiatric Services, a journal of the American Psychiatric Society, "studies have shown that elderly people use prescription drugs three times more frequently than people in the general population. The use of over-the-counter medications among this population is even more extensive, the investigators point out." Thomas L. Patterson of the University of

California at San Diego and co-author of the report, explained to Reuters: "We can expect to see more people over 65 with abuse problems in the coming decades, with the resulting impact on treatment programs and other resources, which are not geared to address the special needs of this age group."

Another short article recently published in *Discover Magazine* (August 1999), "When pills kill" by Tony Dajer, reports a couple of interesting facts. The first stated that a study in the Journal of the American Medical Association revealed that in 1998 an estimated 106,000 Americans died in hospitals from drug side effects. Those were expected side effects, not due to mistaken dosage. Bruce Goldberg adds to this number another "98,000 Americans, who are killed every year by 'medical errors', the vast majority of which were mistakes in prescribing, mixing, or administering drugs" [Alternative Medicine—March 2000]. "When the total number of deaths is calculated, the use of prescription drugs is this country's third leading cause of death," concludes Goldberg. The second fact noted that for high blood pressure alone, there are now 65 drugs plus 29 combination pills, each with its own generic and brand names. According to Reuters Health (August 1999), total retail prescription drug sales are expected to exceed $121.6 billion in 1999. This is an 18 percent rise over last year according to projections released by the National Association of Chain Drug Stores (NACDS). Over the counter medications are expected to achieve sales of $32 billion in 1999 in community pharmacies, up 8.3 percent from last year.

Meanwhile more and more cases are coming to light of the problems related to so-called natural and safe herbal remedies. In August 1999, Reuters Health reported that Chinese herbal remedies used to treat eczema appear to be the cause of rapidly progressive kidney failure in two British women. The World Health Organization (WHO) estimates that 4 billion people (80 percent of the world population) presently use herbal medication for some aspect of primary health care. In articles about illness and injuries in the FDA Consumer Report (September-October 1998), I noted the following listed herbal ingredients and their possible health hazards:

Comfrey—Possible health hazard: obstruction of blood flow to the liver, possibly leading to death.

Willow Bark—Possible health hazards: Reye Syndrome, a potentially fatal disease associated with aspirin intake in children; with chickenpox or flu symptoms, there are allergic reactions in adults. Willow Bark is marketed as an aspirin-free product although actually it contains an ingredient that converts to the same active ingredient as aspirin.

Wormwood—Possible health hazards: neurological symptoms characterized by numbness of the legs and arms, loss of intellect, delirium and paralysis.

These are just a few samples of what has been recognized already with so-called "natural safe herbal ingredients." Stephen Barrett, M.D., a board member of the National Council Against Health Fraud, advises the public to be aware of products that "claim that the supplement has only benefits and no side effects." A product "potent enough to help people, will be potent enough to cause side effects" Barrett says. On March 19, 2000, Guy Gugliotta reported in The Washington Post that "mounting evidence suggests that increasing number of Americans are falling seriously ill or even dying after taking dietary supplements that promise everything from extra energy to sounder sleep". On June 18, 2000, Gugliotta added to his initial report that "dietary supplements companies have begun aggressively targeting children and parents as consumers of their products, among them powerful chemicals designed to help kids gain strength, lose weight or treat illnesses ranging from colds and flu to depression and even attention deficit disorder. As a result, increasing numbers of children are swallowing supplements, often with the knowledge, urging and even insistence of parents in search of 'natural' remedies or 'healthy' alternatives for youngsters who eat too many cupcakes or drink too much soda". Gugliotta continues by warning that "unlike pharmaceutical firms, supplements companies are not required by law to report serious products problems to the government . . . Although some products may be helpful, the surge in supplement use by children and adolescents is causing rising alarm among pediatricians, children's health advocates and federal and state medical officials. At the least, many of the products may be useless. At the worst, some may be dangerous, they say. Supplements are largely untested and unregulated. The full short- and long-term impact of these substances on young bodies is virtually unknown. And in some cases, there's evidence they may be harmful." In an article published also in The Washington Post on April 25, 2000, Lawrence Lindner states "an individual's vulnerability often comes from being uncomfortable, fatigued or overweight for many years, all of which may increase desperation for relief. And desperation opens the door to the idea that 'anything is better than nothing,' Barrett comments. In addition, quacks are not always liars. Frequently, they truly believe in what they're selling... 'Very few people who sell nutrition supplements can be counted on as a reliable source of advice,' Barrett says... The American Dietetic Association sees it the same way, citing 'recommendations made to help sell a product' as one of its '10 Red Flags of Junk Science". In Europe, the European Commission is also showing concerns about the safety of vitamins and supplements. "For those who require supplements, we must make sure that the chemical substances used to produce vitamins and mineral supplements are safe," said David Byrne, EU Health and Consumer safety Commissioner (Reuters – May 2000). These reports clearly show that neither pharmaceuticals nor natural products can be guaranteed to be 100 percent safe.

Let's put aside for a moment pharmaceutical products and alternative healing products. Most physicians are taught in medical school that many illnesses are self-limiting. This means patients often get better on their own. It implies that self-healing has always been recognized within medicine. There is much confusion about what the term "alternative healing" means. Generally speaking, it means any treatment outside the usually accepted medical therapies for disease process. Alternative healing recognizes and accepts the concept "holistic." Broadly speaking, holistic means to treat the whole person, including such facets as diet and lifestyle, as well as the emotional, physical and spiritual elements in a person's life. The aim is to bring all of these into harmony and balance.

The emergence of holistic practice has brought humanity a step further towards self-healing, a positive step indeed. In fact a recent study at Harvard Medical School shows that 4 out of 10 Americans now rely on some type of alternative treatment. Still, we have not yet moved far enough along the road of our self-healing journey. Deepak Chopra and Andrew Weil, to name but two of the most popular authors, have brought less rigid ideas and more of a holistic approach to modern medicine, which is opening doors for everyone. The next step is to go beyond traditional and non-traditional thought on the subject of healing, even beyond "holistic." We can then accept healing without the use of pharmaceutical or natural herbal remedies.

The theme of this book is that an individual can use the keys that exist within themselves to promote self-healing and can bring this practice into being, as a major part of a new lifestyle. Self-healing is using the body's own natural healing process; it also involves understanding why we become ill and imbalanced in the first place. It is learning to dig more deeply into understanding ourselves and into the choices that we make, to be well or to be ill. This must be the next step forward as we head towards a society where there no longer exists the desire or the space for illness, disease and pain.

A choice to heal—Taking back power

Life, we realize, is full of choices: what to eat, what to wear, where to go for lunch, what to watch on television, when to go to bed. We have so many choices to make. Everyday life can make us feel that the choices are so numerous and varied that we become blasé about them. For those of you who don't feel as if you have any choices, just sit down and make a list of the choices you have each day, and you will be surprised. Many times, we choose to give away our power of choice, saying "I don't care," "It's up to you," "It's not important," "You tell me." The words come easily. We give power away to the degree that we believe that there are other people who know better than we do about what is right for us. You may argue that the professionals we consult are educated in specific areas, and we accept their advice because we believe they know better than we do. These people are supposed to have knowledge and experience that we do not possess. Yes, there is a degree of truth in this. But we have now reached the point where we take vitamins, herbs, medication, and even accept surgery that we do not totally understand or necessarily need, because we are told that it is right for us to do so. We go along with this despite the fact that many mistakes are made by those who are in charge.

Millions of patients are taking cocktails of medications which they know little, if anything, about. One of my case studies includes an elderly couple who carried a bag of different pills and medications that they had been taking for so long they had both forgotten what they were prescribed for in the first place. They had no idea what was working and what was not. This was blind faith, to say the least.

On occasion, many of us have declined certain medications or other treatments recommended by a professional based on nothing more than a strong feeling. Usually, we find that we were absolutely right. The good news is that more and more people are returning to believing in their own feelings. However, there are not nearly enough of us yet. It is very easy to see why. For years, we have been bombarded by constant media campaigns that tell us what we need and cannot or should not do without. But even when things appear to work for others, it does not mean that they should or will work for us. We have reached the point of saturation. Every other commercial advertisement on TV is about health and some new wonder pill. It's difficult to open a magazine without finding yet another miraculous cure. This is good as it enables us to perceive more clearly the total ridiculousness of the healthcare situation and gives us a push, a wake up call, encouraging us to think for ourselves and trust our own feelings once again.

Think about it this way: Each and every time you believe in something, anything, outside of yourself, you give away more of you and believe less in yourself. It makes sense then to be discerning when giving away your power. This does not mean that you should not take advice or accept help, but the final choice and decision is yours to make. So take back your power of choice.

When you are sick or ill no matter how seriously, or for how long, you always have a choice to change the situation (that is, if the body has not totally degenerated), and to become well once again. We hear of people who have been diagnosed as terminally ill, given no chance of recovery at all, and yet have made the choice not to accept the situation and have gone on to recover. Amazing things can and do happen. These people are no different from you or me. They simply made the choice to take back their power and heal.

When I see people who are very ill, I look first at where they are within themselves. If they have decided to die or to remain ill, I begin to ascertain if this is really what they want. They may be basing their decision to remain ill or die on a limited perception of their own life. It is possible to bring forward clarity and information whereby they see that there is a reason to live, something to go on for, and then they often do decide to get well.

Two of the case studies in chapter 10 tell the stories of a woman and a man who chose not to get well and the reasons why. Much as we love those close to us, if a person chooses not to get well, we need to accept that choice, and deal with whatever it brings to us. We hold onto life, as we know it, very closely and dearly. But when faced with somebody who wants to let go and no longer wishes to live, it can be a positive experience which enables us to expand our own view of life and death, and our own views of holding on and letting go. So there are valuable lessons for all of us from even seemingly tragic situations.

Believing you have the power to heal is a fact waiting to be accepted. It is also a feeling and a knowing that you will need to let grow. You will also need to become aware of and examine the origins of anything that tells you otherwise. This is the first basic step in taking back your own power and knowing you have a choice to heal. This is what this book is all about. Remember that no established thoughts, facts, figures, or even millions of other people telling you differently are more real or valid than this statement: You have the choice to heal and, furthermore, you can heal yourself. Now, the only thing stopping you from healing yourself is belief, commitment, making decisions, and knowing how. This is an exciting prospect. Remember that today really is the first day of the rest of your life.

Chapter 2

Present Day Healing and Healthcare

❧

Do you remember a few years ago when it seemed like life was moving at a slower pace? Individuals were more open to expressing themselves. They had more time and took more time for themselves and others. Today, the pace of life is becoming faster and faster. However, in the healing, self-healing and wellness movement there is already a shift in the number of people who are committed to being responsible for their own health and wellness. On the other hand, there are also millions of people who feel powerless to act and to do whatever it takes for them to make the switch and become aware and responsible for their wellness.

In many ways this is understandable when you have a lifestyle based on the same routine day after day. You have a family to take care of with all the responsibilities that go with paying the bills, and keeping a job. It is easy to allow yourself to feel that you do not have time, and to let yourself become programmed by advertising campaigns which clearly tell you what you need and must have in order to survive within that programmed existence. It seems quite natural then to put your health and wellness into other people's hands. In short, it may seem easier to believe what we want to hear and to find quick fixes to our health crisis. Incidentally, words often included in advertising of health products include "breakthrough," "magical," "miracle cures," "new discovery," "detoxify," "purify" and "energize." The FDA guide to Dietary Supplements warns that consumers need to be on the lookout for fraudulent products and reminds everyone that the term "natural" doesn't guarantee that a product is safe. "Think of poisonous mushrooms. They are natural," says Elizabeth Yetley, Director of FDA's Office of Special Nutritionals. "As with all products on the market," Yetley continues, "consumers need to be discriminating. FDA and industry have important roles to play, but consumers must take responsibility, too."

Pharmaceutical companies, as we see from the latest statistics, have never before spent so much money on advertising. Millions of people take drugs expecting them to work in often sure-fire and miraculous ways because they have been told that they will and have accepted the statistics presented to them. People often believe that a product must be good and worth a try if it has been clinically tested, researched by doctors and scientists and perhaps even used widely over a long period of time "outside of the country." But the fact also remains that science and medicine are not infallible. Further down the road we hear of the horror stories about the long-term adverse negative reactions and effects of these same drugs that were once hailed as miraculous.

When we really look at the vast number of people who are still consuming pharmaceutical medication, natural medication and supplements, we realize that these people are giving away their belief in the body's natural ability to heal, and accepting answers from outside of themselves.

Why is this still going on? If we stand back and look at

the evolution of the human species, it might appear that in many ways we are presently evolving at a high speed. There is a lot going on and changing within us that we feel we cannot relate to or even express to ourselves and others. It is also a wondrous time as we each experience our own individual shifts in consciousness and awareness. Sometimes, we feel that we are opening up more to ourselves and to those around us, finding that we can connect more easily with those we feel are on our wavelength, perhaps even more so than ever before. However, there too can be an even greater sense of aloneness and isolation, which may feel more intensely than ever before. For many people in this time, there will be a sense of faded and blurred perception as we have experiences, feelings, thoughts and realizations that we have never had before, and that do not fit in with what we know. At times, this might even feel like we are going a little crazy or losing our grip on reality. However, this is a period of adjustment and a natural part of the process happening in our present time. Our comfort zones are being stretched and challenged again and again, but remember, we do have the answers to our own questions and are capable of finding them even without outside help.

Meanwhile the media will continue to bring us news of more and more predicted future health crises, and more miracle health cures. Both of these factors, crises and cures, are trends that will continue to grow and become more intense, before the situation finally levels out. Even the most accepting persons among us will begin to question the saturation point and ridiculousness of the overall healthcare situation.

For example, we have been told over and over again that the food grown on our planet is no longer giving us what our bodies need because of mass production, freezing, storing, and the use of chemicals and pesticides. Furthermore, we are told that our water is contaminated by natural and unnatural pollutants and that the air we breathe is dangerous. It is no wonder that so many people are convinced that they must take pills and supplements, and use lotions and all kinds of other products to negate the effects of the modern world and modern living. Because of this indoctrination, many people now believe that they cannot live and reach their true potential without vitamins and supplements.

But just how deeply do we need to take these facts and figures into account? If we accept this picture of current reality from others, we may feel bleak and powerless, even fearful. Let's step back here for a moment. Any person who has lived in the mountains or by the ocean and then moved to a busy smog-filled city will tell you that they adjusted to their new environment and were not stricken with illness. We may not be living a life filled with the same "good, homegrown, wholesome foods" that our grandparents ate, or the "cleaner air" that they breathed, but at the same time, why do we have so little belief in the ability of our bodies to adjust on their own without the help of so many outside products? Isn't it time to get back in touch with our bodies by giving them the chance to show us what they can do?

Let us look again for a moment at the mind and our belief systems. We have long heard of the placebo effect used in the medical and healing fields. A group of people with the same health problems are split in two groups: one group is given standard medication for their condition and the other group is given a sugar-coated tablet, known as a placebo, that contains no medication. This second group is unaware that they are being given a placebo. Later the two groups are tested. Amazingly, it is found that both groups respond in positive ways to their separate treatments. We may wonder: if the patient heals as well using a placebo tablet by believing that he or she is taking medication, could it be that medication itself works as well as it does because we believe that it will?

Recently, the placebo technique has also been used in

surgery, as reported on August 23, 1999, by the Houston Chronicle in an article entitled "Sham Surgery." The article presents a study by Bruce Moseley, an orthopedic surgeon and clinical associate professor at Baylor College of Medicine, who was skeptical about a commonplace operation performed on older patients' knees. The following is an extract of the article:

The patients suffered from osteoarthritis, a crippling, irreversible condition in which the cartilage covering the bones has worn away with age. It is the major cause of mobility loss among the elderly.

Arthroscopy surgery, in which doctors work through tiny incisions using a "scope" to see, is effective in repairing torn cartilage from injuries. However, it cannot replace the missing cartilage in arthritic patients; doctors can only wash out the joint and scrape, or debride, the rough spots.

Yet nearly everyone said their arthritic knee pain decreased after surgery. The question was, why?

In an unusual, groundbreaking study, Moseley and other Houston researchers are comparing actual surgery to phony, or placebo surgery to see whether the operation really helps or if people simply believe it relieves their pain[. . .]

Initially, Moseley, who is best known as the team physician for the Houston Rockets, was interested in comparing the benefits of rinsing and scraping the knee joint vs. rinsing alone. He suspected that washing away debris was what gave people relief.

When Dr. Nelda Wray, an internist who runs a research unit financed by Baylor College of Medicine and Veterans Affairs, suggested that they also look at the placebo effect, Moseley was taken aback.

He said, "What do you mean placebo? This is

surgery!" Moseley said. "The more we learned about it, the more we realized surgery may have the strangest placebo effect of any intervention."

A pilot study of 10 patients yielded intriguing results. Five of the patients received placebo surgery, just three shallow nicks on their skin so their knees would look like those of the other patients.

Two years after sham surgery, patients reported the same amount of relief from pain and swelling as those who had had the real operation. Four of the five placebo patients said the surgery was so worthwhile that they would recommend it to a friend. One patient even requested the operation be repeated on the other knee.

"We know from the medical literature on the placebo effect that it is a significant effect, and the amount of the effect is greater with the magnitude of the placebo," Wray said. "If the pill is bigger, you'll measure a bigger effect."

Wray suspects that people get better just from an encounter with a surgeon. The white lab coat, the dramatic setting, the declaration of "I'm going to make you better" have a powerful effect.

It is likely that more experimentation and research will take place before conclusions are reached, but the topic of the placebo effect must at least ignite a spark of interest. Once again, we may wonder: if the patient heals as well after a "sham surgery," could it be that surgery at times works as well as it does because we believe that it will? How big a part then does belief play in our own self-healing process? It is clear that when we believe that we are getting help and being treated, we heal.

A look at alternative medicine
There are many healing therapies, techniques, services,

and experiences available today. Look in your telephone book or on the Internet and search for associations, institutions and centers of alternative medicine, and holistic practices. On the Internet, Yahoo lists 43 alternative therapies at the time of writing this book. Health insurances are slowly bowing to demand and some people are finding that their health insurance coverage will pay for some of the basics such as acupuncture, massage, counseling, polar therapy, and reflexology.

We can group alternative therapies mainly in six categories: products, machines, experiences, master-oriented, release clearing, and awareness. Different ways work for different people at different times, and credentials and diplomas are not always a guarantee of excellence. The wisest way to choose something new for yourself is to question practitioners about how their particular service works. Ask questions and make sure you have an understanding of what you can realistically expect from each session. Although alternative therapies can offer very different pathways, they are all connected and headed in the same direction. The prime purposes are to heal, to inspire, to awaken, to empower, to release, to direct, to disclose, to focus, to realize, to accept, and to give. They are here to remind us of the greatness of our being and that we are in control.

Alternative therapies also offer people the basics such as a time period where they focus completely on themselves, fulfilling needs such as touch, and the feeling of being important, understood and supported. These feelings are important for all of us; they help us gain greater confidence and a growing awareness of ourselves. I have included in chapter 10 the story of a woman who had healing sessions, not primarily to be healed, but to be touched and understood. When she had these needs fulfilled, she went on in due course to heal herself.

Alternative therapies and experiences are often the only avenues that some people feel they have open to them, where they feel they can be safe and express themselves without being judged or ridiculed. As already mentioned, alternative therapies can be found relatively easily in all areas. Let's look briefly at just three of them: LaStone therapy, the flotation tank and the sweat lodge.

LaStone therapy is relatively new. It's offered by The British School of Complementary Therapy. A session consists of a light massage using aromatherapy massage oil and hot smooth stones of lava rock, which are placed under the spine and also on energy points throughout the body such as the stomach, chest and forehead. Apparently, one stroke of the lump of lava is equivalent to 10 regular massage strokes. Why are lava rocks used? Their natural smoothness and denseness mean that they hold heat very well, which relaxes, nurtures, and removes pain and tension from the body. Also, the LaStone therapy can be used with ice-cold frozen stones to treat a specific injury. A session typically lasts 75 minutes.

Flotation tanks provide an experience that can be wonderfully freeing and nurturing, as long as you feel fine being in an enclosed space. The session consists of going inside a flotation tank, an enclosed space that is big enough for you to spread out your entire body. You lie down in inches of body temperature warm water, which has a very high concentration of sea salt. It's like being in the Dead Sea: you float effortlessly. Most chambers offer a neck pillow to rest and support your head. Some offer soft music or aromatherapy fragrances. The chamber can be completely dark or a small light might be included. This can be turned on and off by the individual from the inside of the chamber. Apart from being very relaxing and nurturing, a flotation tank helps you to get away from the stress and strain of the everyday world and enter for a while a womb-like state. It's a great experience for letting go and getting back in touch with you.

The mind also relaxes, as there is an element of sensory deprivation, a lack of visual and audio stimulation. Many people swear by flotation tanks as a way to get in touch with their own creative thought process, to find and develop new ideas and to solve past and present issues. Flotation tanks were once very popular and have enjoyed a resurge in popularity in both the United States and Europe during the past few years.

The Native American sweat lodge can have a similar clearing, nurturing, revitalizing and spiritually progressive effect. However, during my last visit to an Indian reservation, the Native Americans explained that they use the sweat lodge more as a sauna for the body and as a time of prayer, rather than for any esoteric purposes that alternative and new age groups seem to find in them.

A sweat lodge consists of a construction made often of wood or mud, built outside in a peaceful place. The construction is big enough for up to 10 people to sit inside. It can be made from branches of trees or built with wood, covered by more branches or tarpaulin, or mud and sand. Large, round, smooth stones are heated outside and then brought inside the lodge and placed one by one in a corner. Inside the lodge, it is dark. It certainly feels like a sauna and is very quiet and peaceful. Similar to a flotation tank, the benefits and experience is often profound.

Over the past few years, sweat lodges have increased in popularity amongst holistic and New Age groups. These groups have created and are offering their own adaptation of the original experience.

There are so many different therapies and healing modalities available right now. I am not suggesting that you necessarily need any of them, but it might be useful to your own self-healing process to be aware of what is available now. All of these options are ways and paths that you have connections with already within yourself, and you can adapt them to use in your own way if you choose. For example, you could take a course or workshop on conscious singing or you could simply think about singing, find your own voice and start to bring that aspect into your life. You might take a creative writing or art class, or you could also get some materials and sit down with a blank piece of paper, pencils or colors and simply let yourself go and put down on paper whatever comes to you. You will find some more of yourself in the process. Remember your writing or art does not have to be anything in particular but an expression of you in that moment. Move away from the idea that you cannot write or cannot draw. Instead, let go and let whatever comes come.

The same applies to musical instruments. Music is inside of you. Take an instrument you feel most comfortable with and allow yourself to play and see what happens. Do not believe that you cannot or that you must play in a particular way. Be your own psychoanalyst, draw shapes, lines, and doodles on a piece of paper. Let things come. Then sit back and ask yourself what is the inner part of you expressing amongst those shapes, lines and doodles. Check and re-check your answers. But remember at some point you need to accept and believe in your own answers and insights.

Feng-Shui is offered as a popular service nowadays. Feng-Shui is the Chinese art of placement. You can have an expert visit your office or house and move around your furniture and belongings following Feng-Shui principles. According to one practitioner, this requires the combined skills of architectural interior design, geomancy environmental psychology and client participation. You could read one of the many books on the subject or in my opinion, best of all, you could simply throw away everything that is broken or that you no longer need to create space for yourself. Then check your furniture and belongings. Feel where different pieces need to be placed. Then move things around. You might be amazed at how you instinctively already know exactly where everything needs to be, intuitively knowing and feeling what will work best for you in your individual environment.

Recently I have noticed supermarkets advertising fresh flowers as "food for the soul." I could not agree more. Both men and women are treating themselves more and more with fresh flowers for home and the office. Thankfully, flowers are no longer seen as a predominantly female item; men are allowing themselves to enjoy flowers too. Plants in the office or home bring their own magic as well as create more oxygen. Flowers and plants do not have to be expensive. You could grow your own, pick some wild ones, or swap and recycle plants among friends.

Tai Chi is another interesting discipline to be used for both physical and mental health. Again you might go to a class, read a book or rent a video, but don't get stuck on getting the moves right because they are all there already waiting inside of you. A part of you is already a Tai Chi master waiting to come out. Close the blinds or drapes. Put on some soft music that feels right for you. Start with a little gentle stretching and then begin to move slowly. Get comfortable with your moves. Let your body flow and take you in the directions that it wants to go. Do what feels good for you. Later you may feel like moving in this way outside and consciously incorporating deep breathing into your session. Trust yourself. Find yourself again in movement.

The list of alternative medicine, healing therapies and experiences goes on and on and will continue to grow. You can choose to feel overwhelmed by it or enjoy it and enjoy yourself within all of the possibilities. In short, it's playtime. As you discover new ways to express yourself, to play, to grow, to clear and to heal, remember that although there are many masters, you are a master too.

Chapter 3

Nothing is Ever
Only as It Seems

✧

Reality and you

There is a lot of fear in the world today. Many people worry about a possible World War III involving chemical and nuclear weapons. Others are concerned that the end of the world is imminent, or that life as we know it will end. Still others are close to panic, feeling helpless and out of control. We have the choice to feel this way, but we can also take another path if we wish. It is important to realize that when we learn to heal ourselves, we are not limited merely to changing our own realities; the world reality is also ours to change. We are all responsible for the collective thoughts and fears. In fact, each time we allow ourselves the thought that catastrophes may happen, that everything will fall apart, and that the world is going to be destroyed, we feel powerless to do anything and we give up our unique strength. In essence, we are as responsible as those that drop the bombs and pull the triggers. While we continue to accept war, violence and horror, our own fascination with the subject helps to create it. The choice and the responsibility are there for each and every one of us to use. As you change your lifestyle and create your own self-healing lifestyle, you will begin to realize more and more that you are not insignificant or unimportant, but a powerful and amazing being. Any limitations that you accept are of your own choosing. The perfect reality is possible where everyone can live together if they choose, a world where there is no hunger, no violation, no abuse. It is not a dream out of our reach. It is a conscious choice that we each have the option to make. Future reality is ours to create; it's part of our new self-healing, new lifestyle choice.

Changing beliefs and re-examining security

It seems that from time beyond our remembrance, mankind has needed to believe in something greater than himself. Faith in something outside of ourselves and greater than ourselves has helped and continues to help many people to grow and expand. It also offers enormous comfort and support in times of trouble. It is the basic right of each and every individual to believe in whatever form of higher being they choose. It is also the basic right of each individual to have the choice not to believe in any greater power than oneself. Sadly, people have a tendency to make others like themselves, and in some societies faiths and beliefs are not allowed to remain a matter of personal choice. How many people have ever really questioned what a belief is, how it occurs, or why we hold onto it? Society does not make it easy for anyone who thinks differently. Perhaps that is why few people appear to think very deeply.

We might agree that we have been, in many ways, collectively taken in by the shallow promises of success, trading our uniqueness for false security and materialism. We accept whole-heartedly the belief that our body will grow old, cease to function well and finally, within a particular time-frame, die. This belief is a deep-rooted concept as old as our memory, or the memory that we believe in. Yet we are capable of other memories of other times when this concept was not the only reality. Generally, we dismiss these thoughts of other possibilities and realities, even if they do occur to us. Our belief system is strong so we get what we believe, which can be very little. Almost all human beings have been indoctrinated with rigid concepts that define the society they form. Most believe that their answers will come from outside sources. Some believe that many lifetimes are spent living what appears to be a haphazard series of events. Often people imagine death as a dark, empty space at the end of so-called life, and accept this black and white, limited concept as reality.

Another way to experience and validate our life is to use the mind and create lines and sequences of logical events, and to use reasoning as our thought process, so that everything makes sense. This way of thinking does not go far enough. It doesn't explain healing, for example, which does not always make rational sense, although it does happen and can be observed.

Some people take thinking a step further, expanding on all they know and do not know, reaching what seems to be the point of completion, where questions and answers are no longer necessary. This is a blissful place. But how many bemoan the fact that they cannot stay there? They believe at first that "this is it," the ultimate awareness. Then later, they become disillusioned with the realization that life is constantly moving and bringing ups and downs, highs and lows, taking them away from what had seemed perfection. Consciousness cannot and does not end in that state of completion after all. We are multi-dimensional beings. People who have reached this state of completion and then moved on have not failed in their search for awareness, but merely become disillusioned with what appears to be endless. The positive part of that particular pathway is the wonderful realization of the interconnectedness of the self with all other beings, time, places and events.

There is also the path of the fatalist. These people do not believe in self, but only in outside sources and answers, in a perfect order, perhaps even fate. This path takes away the need to ponder on that which seems so complex. They just "go with the flow," regardless of how much pain and suffering this path brings. This pathway can be also validated with sentiment such as "no pain, no gain."

Today in the more affluent countries, many people are taking the opportunity to think in different ways and to question what has always been accepted. But the process seems very slow. Human nature wishes for change, but is generally afraid or feels threatened by change. How many years have we spent existing within false securities to realize too late that there is no security at all? We are born alone and we die alone. Yet many people spend their lives trying to avoid aloneness and loneliness. I believe there is no real security except within ourselves, and yet that security is endless. I also believe that we are beings with vast potential, and that we do not need to be kept in order by fear. We are capable of knowing and doing what is right for ourselves and others.

Humanity is slowly moving on. There are some thinkers amongst us who have new ideas and are prepared to go beyond all that has ever been known, experienced, believed or conceived before. They do not accept that there is nothing new under the sun. Ideas such as the ability of man to fly or to harness electricity and invent television, might have seemed strange years ago, but this didn't stop them from becoming a reality. Even now, voices that are different may be hushed or ridiculed, but their time will come too. This is inevitable. These people, who dare to be different and go beyond ideas of the past, are indeed our future. They open doorways in the consciousness of us all, to ideas beyond what has already been realized.

The idea of reality created by past philosophers and thinkers such as Plato, Aristotle, and more recently Freud and Einstein has been little challenged or changed, except by a select few. In some cases it has been followed blindly for thousands of years. This is quite understandable, when you think that so many people are too busy earning the basic necessities for life to have time or even the inclination to really think.

Einstein said: "They are two ways to live your life. One is as though there are no miracles, the other is as though everything is a miracle." This shows us that he too recognized that there is more than one reality and way of life. Many people cannot envision enough belief in themselves to realize that they are just as capable of having original thoughts, and that they could go beyond all that is currently being accepted by mankind. "Concepts, which have been proved to be useful in ordering things easily, acquire such an authority over us that we forget their human origin and accept them as invariable." wrote Einstein. Humanity at large is based on the thought patterns of a few, and barely changes, even when it appears to do so. But on the positive side, people are now beginning to want to believe in themselves, and to reclaim the power they thought was lost, only to discover that it was there all of the time. The huge sales of self-help books and motivational tapes, and the popularity of self-development classes and available hands-on experiences, as well as the ever-growing New Age movement, are confirming this change.

Creating our world

Many people now find it acceptable to believe that they co-create with a higher power. This is the first, big step towards realizing the greatness of ourselves. Of course it seems a big responsibility to stand alone and accept the fact that you do know exactly what you are doing at all times, that you have made no mistakes, that everything is interconnected and perfect, that everything that happens with and to you is up to you, and as much as you created it you can change it. This is a more comfortable thought for many people to believe than the idea that life is beyond our power and imagination, or that fate is all. For those who still cling to the old ideas, let me point out that more and more we are being urged to go beyond our "comfort zone" now. I am not suggesting that there is any right or wrong here, only that there are always more choices than most people realize, even when situations seem totally impossible, and that whatever is actually happening, we each have agreed to and had a part in creating.

Many of the so-called New Age thinkers believe that the higher self knows what it is doing and if something painful is happening, it must be karma, a kind of punishment for past actions and events. Again, this is basically the fatalistic approach, the concept that pain must be experienced, the popular "no pain no gain" view. Of course there is value in all of these ways and they are all there to be experienced and expressed, but there is no need to be bound or stuck in any one of them. We always have a choice to bring change to ourselves and to do things differently.

Another place where many people become lost is the belief that they have to be good or important, that they must and should behave in a good and loving manner. So they continue to live life in self-sacrificing ways, feeling that if they just love enough, everything will be all right. Sadly, many see that this does not work yet at this moment in time, because we are not all together at the same point in our reality. So these people continue to be hurt, and never understand why.

We often tend to believe we are not doing or being enough, and we immediately blame ourselves first, instead of standing back and taking a much bigger picture into account. This is where knowing yourself is most important. How do you act and react? How much do you empathize with others? Really start to listen to yourself and others. Fulfill your needs. Go with what you feel, and take into account everything that you have experienced in the past. How is all of that past shaping your present reality? Look beyond your own concept of what the past is. See all the many different people who make up who you are, young, old, male, female, the different races and cultures, even alien beings, and all the parts of you that we do not even have words to describe, or feelings to relate to, because they are outside of what we know. All of this is "you." We are capable of seeing and knowing ourselves in all of our splendor and of knowing others too, and what we call life in all of its many different forms and expressions. It does not mean that we need to be aware or looking at every moment of the day. But at least to look often or even from time to time, and to look more closely than we do presently, because the more we look, the more we will find ourselves. We will then begin to realize that we are not being one person, one force, good or bad, higher or lower, but a rich, deep tapestry with many faces, realities and dimensions. As we continue this process, we begin to see that we are capable, powerful, perfect and indeed indestructible, that life and death are neither beginnings nor ends. We begin to see that life can be quite wonderful, a joyful, wondrous, exciting and often challenging experience. We see that we are not victims after all in anything, but rather consenting participants. Life then becomes exciting and filled with hope rather than despair.

Basic concepts and values such as "do to others what you would have them do unto you," and "care about all living things," are noble sentiments, but only when we each truly love, value, care and accept ourselves. Then it is easy to be generous with others. Without a doubt, what you most dislike in others, you also dislike in yourself. Take this a step further. Explore the parts of you that you dislike and see where they come from and where they are going. This is healing. It is also time to take a look at our own core belief system. As we embrace self-healing, we may realize that our goal may not be after all to be all that we can be, but rather to be all that we already are.

Finding your own time

Looking closely then, at who you think you are and how reality is, you see that things are never only as they seem. We are multidimensional beings. These are not just words, for at any moment, we are an endless number of different people, many we have been and many we have yet to become. To open your perception, you will need to look at the idea of time itself. There is the time that we all abide by, agree to, live by, morning to evening, day by day, minute to minute. Then there is our own time. It is necessary to have a real feeling of your own time. I include in chapter 9 a simple "sitting down and being still" exercise so that you can feel and know your own time for yourself. When you take the step of removing watches and clocks from your reality, you can connect even more with your own time. After a while, you will find yourself knowing what the actual time is to the minute without watches or clocks and without being disconnected from your own time. Like everything else, the time and the speed at which we are vibrating are unique to each one of us. It can be a wonderful experience to discover your own speed and time and then to recognize other people's. By doing so, you will allow yourself to be open to other realities as valid as the one you have always felt was solid and complete, realizing that other realities are also part of your life.

As I write this chapter, I am sitting outside. It is a beautiful summer early morning. The birds are singing. I take a break from my work and I watch a blackbird that has landed nearby. I hear the blackbird sneeze. I am amazed. As if for confirmation, the bird sneezes again. Twice I think, "Wow, I had not realized that a blackbird might sneeze." The next thought strongly enters my mind, "I can speak to dead people." I don't take time to wonder why I have that thought, because I am also known as a medium and talking to dead people is an acceptable fact for me. However, as soon as the thought crosses my mind, I see that a man is kneeling down beside me. He has a gentle presence. He is in the physical form of an Arab with full costume and head-dress. I recognize him right away. It has been a few years since I last saw him and I am happy to see him again. We talk about the book and how I am doing. I feel my heart center open to him. Emotionally I become fluid. It is so good to see him again. He is a part of me and part of a reality in which I have been before, I am now and will always be. We talk a little more and then he leaves. I feel glowing and warmed, enjoying the magic of the moment. I think about all of those moments that led to our conversation just then, the way I stopped what I was doing for a second and allowed myself to be open, to follow my own speed, to forget the schedule, and to notice something new, which was the blackbird sneezing. And then I chose to put myself into another way of being, and to tune in on another wavelength by allowing the strong thought and reaccepting it, even though for me, it was not a new one. The thought was, "I can speak to dead people." Afterwards, I go back to my writing, feeling great and reaffirming within myself how magical and wonderful life is. Letting go can be as simple and immediate as that. Noticing the blackbird sneeze and communicating with a non-physical being came just from a moment of letting go.

I will leave the subject of communicating with the dead for another book. But for now I will say that you too can communicate here and now, and see those you have loved and who now feel separated from. You will need to realize first that there is no separation, no here, and no there, no now and then. This "here and there" is just as much a part of you as is life. The barrier you face, which seems to make this communication difficult or even impossible, is just an accepted and limited concept, a fear. You might be trying too hard to communicate with loved ones, or be blinded by grief. That's why you have doubts about communicating with those who have passed on, and you might say, you have "lost" them.

Nothing is only as it seems

Have you ever been away from home, for say a week or 10 days, and noticed that everything looks and feels different when you return? You may notice objects and shapes that you had stopped noticing before. So to take a break from your present reality, to step out somehow is a good way to get a fresh perspective and to see things as new, or should I say, to see things in the present moment and more of how they actually are. When you are very young, your perception is very different. As small children, we revel in the imagination. But for most of us there comes a point, often starting when we begin school, where we begin to be taught what is real and what is not. We are taught by people doing a job, whether they believe or not in the concepts of the reality they are teaching. Most often, our parents go along with this process. An element of fear drives everyone involved, as no one wants the child not to be able to fit into the accepted reality by which we all live. What might be called an overactive imagination in children is deemed "undesirable," even if the words are not expressed as such. We are taught to be focused in the here and now, to have a firm grip on reality, and to be able to work with the mind in logical directions and patterns. These are all goals to be achieved and then praised for having achieved them. Yet at the same time, we see parents, teachers and others struck with a sense of awe when a child comes out with a statement which is deemed profound yet makes no logical sense. Even though these adults are perpetuating the importance of logical concepts, just for a moment they come back again to be in touch with themselves, as they listen with wonder to a child's profound, wise and magical thoughts. A child's imagination is often seen as wondrous, enjoyed from time to time, but is many times stifled and kept firmly in its place. It is no surprise that as adults many of us have difficulty in letting go and allowing our imagination to run free when we do give ourselves that freedom.

A child's reality is full of colors and vibrations, unformed thoughts all going on at the same time. And it is the same for all of us as adults, even if we are not aware of it. In early childhood it is clearer, simply because before a certain age is reached, and the mind begins to "make sense" of the fabulous and rich array of senseless matter, we see things how they are. The sense comes into play as we begin to learn, and are taught, that this is black and this is white. From then on, we accept that what we believe is order. In many ways, we stop looking and seeing. We no longer really look at a chair or a flower. We have no need to. We already believe we know exactly what it is. We have been told what it is and then later have told ourselves many times just what that object is, so we stop looking. Then we begin to believe that nothing is new, that there is nothing to look at. It could be many years later when perhaps for a moment we step out of our conditioning and happen to notice that a flower is giving off a light or subtle energy, that it feels and moves, and is very much alive. Then we are once again delighted and somehow surprised that we did not notice it before, yet this flower was always there to be noticed. We had just stopped looking.

Each and every day we have a choice of how to be and how to perceive reality. Yet most of the time we just go along with life and are not particularly aware. Reality even becomes boring and usual, made stale by custom, and also totally solid somehow. We may even feel imprisoned by that solidness. We search for things out there, things that are different and have other meanings, not even noticing all that is around us and before our very own eyes, because we simply stopped looking and seeing a long time ago. We grow also to see our lives and ourselves in very fixed ways. We grow to believe what we see is the sum total of us and how everything is. We become blasé. At times our perception can become so narrow that what we see is a very small picture indeed.

Opening up

To develop further awareness of who you are and where you are at any particular moment, try this short exercise. Ask yourself: "Where am I right now?" If you are standing in the kitchen doing the dishes or driving along in your car concentrating on the road, your first answer will be: "I am standing in the kitchen doing the dishes," or, "I am driving my car." Now ask yourself: "Where else am I?" Be aware that your mind may also be with someone else, your husband, one of the children, a friend you spoke with earlier, perhaps in events that happened yesterday, last week, or even years ago. You might also be at a planned weekend that you are looking forward to in the future, at a party, or in the distant future seeing how life is going to be for you then. Could this be an explanation for déjà vu? We are already living and seeing the future now and sometimes we remember certain parts, a face, or a conversation.

These are just two small examples of other times and places where you are probably at, at the same moment, as well as where you already know you are right now. There are many more. You can develop this awareness even further by asking yourself again: "Where else am I also right now at this moment besides the past and the future?" You might find yourself being aware that you are in quite an unfamiliar setting, wearing clothes that you do not know and do not recognize. And you may even see yourself being a person that is not like you or anyone you have seen before. If this happens, just accept the process, keep asking yourself more questions, and receive more answers. Some people call this the awareness of "parallel realities." This may be true or it may also be that as we develop and expand our awareness and understanding, we find that "parallel" is a concept as limited as the concept of "linear time" and so-called "straight lines of thought and existence."

We all play many different roles most of the time. You can expand your awareness of this fact by simply stopping for a moment now and ask yourself: "Who am I being right now?" Again, there are endless possibilities. You may be the one in charge, the angry one, the victim, or the winner. Look at the role you are playing and see which face comes to you. Is there a timeframe to that face and being? Is this someone from the past or the future or is he or she timeless? Remember, I use "past," "present" and "future" only as a form of accepted measure, not as any kind of fixed reality. As you develop more and more your own awareness, you will see that you are an amazing actor or actress. You create quite beautiful, sad and dramatic, and even dreadful dramas. We each work in different ways. Some of us prefer drama, some mystery, others comedy. Notice how you play. All of these roles and scenarios are played out in our lives on a daily basis. The field of psychology realizes this, but in a limited way. You do not need a special regime or concept to unravel the mystery of yourself. You just need to ask the questions and believe in your own answers, and to continue developing your awareness. The further you go, the more you will discover how absolutely amazing you are. In fact, television, books, plays and video games pale into insignificance, when you realize that nothing is quite as fascinating and entertaining as you are.

Things are also never "only as they seem" in the area of communication. We are all aware at some time or another of the basics of multidimensional communication. We call it reading between the lines. This may happen as we read a letter, for example. Or if we are talking to someone, we may hear more than what the other person is actually saying. This hearing something else happens, quite literally or otherwise. Communication is present constantly in many shapes and forms. Learning a foreign language can also bring more awareness about communication, as the words and syntax in another language may be very different from what we know, so we pay attention and notice more when we speak initially. As you develop further awareness of your communications, you can become aware of all the different parts and people within you that are talking and being answered by the other person at the same time, and of all the different parts and people that the other person is also communicating to you with.

Writing is another example. No two people who read this chapter will receive exactly the same information from it. Often we read a book and then go back to it later, and understand it in a different way, or even in a more complete way. Perhaps that is why the written word can be so powerful.

There are endless other languages and forms of communications, such as signs and symbols, to name just two. Look for languages within yourself. Remember, if nothing much seems to be going on in your life right now, it only seems that way. So sit back. Take another look; feel, see and become aware more carefully of all that is actually happening, especially at those times when you feel nothing much is going on.

A self-healing story of my own illustrates the fact that sometimes we need to go deeper into ourselves and look more closely at our beliefs and concepts and our own communication.

Everything was going great for me. Life was running

smoothly. I was enjoying good health, as I always have. I never expect to be ill, so I am generally not. One day I was talking to my father on the telephone about healing, encouraging him to keep going with his own self-healing work. Looking back later, I realized his self-doubt. It was almost as if he had said to me, "Well, if you think that you've got it, try this," because within 24 hours I had an abscess on one of my gums above a tooth which seemed in itself perfectly fine. Over the next day or so this abscess developed and I was in pain. And then, worse, the entire right side of my face became quite visibly swollen. My first reaction was fear, because the only area of my body in which I have ever had any problem with is my teeth. I do not like going to the dentist, as I have a real sensitivity to pain (teeth and gums are very connected to the nervous system). As a healer I quickly ruled out the idea of going to the dentist, having total belief that I could heal this myself.

My father lost his teeth at quite a young age due to gum disease. I had always felt that I would choose to have all of my teeth removed rather than have extensive dental work done. So I had two factors to deal with. One was fear that gum disease might be hereditary. Two, I remembered as I looked back, that I had already visualized and accepted having all of my teeth removed and having artificial replacements at some point. So first, I clearly made up my mind I was not going to have gum disease just because my father had. Then I erased the vision of myself with perfect, artificial teeth.

The first day, I worked on releasing the pain of the abscess and was able to focus despite the pain. I considered once taking painkillers, but made up my mind not to do this so I could explore pain further. The next day I worked on the pain and swelling. I used positive thought, letting go, visualization, and directing energy to that particular place. Three to four days later, the swelling was gone, and barely any pain remained. But the white abscess was still there. Now I had a problem because I had a mental block. I could not make it go away. In fact, I had the age-old concept that it would have to be burst and that the poison would have to be drained, released, cleared, or cut for the release to happen. I felt very stuck with this thought and did not know how to proceed. I sat down and asked myself what was it that was blocking me. What was I letting stop me? After a while it came to me. I found myself regressing to a very coarse woman, very loud-mouthed, dirty and poor in the middle-ages. I disliked this woman. I asked myself: "Why? Why do I dislike her so much?" The answer was loud and clear: ignorance. Ah, so there it was, the answer to my block: ignorance. I then visualized myself embracing and loving this woman. I took her into my being and there I released any dislike of her. I realized then that I have always disliked ignorance very much in all states and forms. I have even been fearful of it because I can see how dangerous it is in individuals and society as a whole. This was a turning point in my self-healing process. Within 24 hours the abscess had gone. There was no pain, no need to have it burst or for any poison to be taken out. The situation was cleared.

The master within

There are countless healing books on the market at present, and even more on theories, visualizations, and ways offered to heal yourself. I highly recommend looking into a variety of different pathways and then starting your own healing process with whatever feels right for you at the time. Then expand by becoming aware, listening to yourself, and developing your own workable techniques. The most important thing not to do is to take any one way or regime and say: "This is it!" Because the "this is it" is constantly changing and moving as life is and as you are.

A woman came to see me some time ago for a rebirthing

after a telephone consultation. She was middle-aged, single, and was living in a large house with her father. For six years, she had been following an oriental master who taught a particular kind of yoga. Her master was based in an Asian country. The woman was required to meditate for two hours every day, focusing her attention only on the third eye, the forehead area. She had a prestigious job, which she hated, but kept it because it allowed her the time and money to take regular trips to visit her master in the East. After six years of meditation, she felt she must have a block, as she could still not find a state of peace and stillness within her mind. She was very sad and depressed. She wanted to go to Asia and stay with the master and serve, but the master had refused. The reason was very clear. The master had seen the master in her and wanted her to move on and be the master that she really was. Unfortunately, this master did not explain the workings of his great wisdom. So the woman was confused and unhappy, not knowing what was going on. It was as if there was a spiritual cord that tied her to the master, and she had a great fear of it being severed. The more she clamored for his understanding and support the more she was pushed away.

This woman felt afraid and could not make sense of what was going on. She was shocked and confused because prior to her visit with me, she had begun to experience sexual feelings. She was shocked because this was a part of herself that she had put away years ago, not expecting it ever to return. She was soothed but suspicious when I told her it was all right to have these feelings and that they were not a threat to her. On the contrary, the sexual energy could be used as an ally rather than seen as the enemy, and it could be moved around her body at will by using her mind.

When we met, this woman was the picture of misery. She was a vegetarian, but had not been taking care of her body at all. It was literally starving from a lack of food, love and warmth. I noticed that she had a psychic shield around her. As the session progressed, this shield lifted and the colors of her aura became clearly visible. I asked her later if she had visualized any type of protection before she arrived as I could see that the shield around her was a strong one. She had not, but she explained that at home she slept in a room with pictures of the master on each and every wall. She also carried with her at all times a picture of the master. She mentioned that her master had told her that his protection was always around her. I pointed out that this might be great, but there was a downside: with such a strong protection, it allowed nothing to come into her being and nothing to flow out. So she was in many ways quite cut off and disconnected. As an intelligent person, she could clearly see this truth and agreed to look again at the situation and perhaps to make some changes and visualizations of her own protection. This would allow an inward and outward flow, whereby she would no longer be so disconnected from the outside, others and herself.

The woman, although privileged in many ways throughout her life, had a very demanding and dominating father who had set unrealistically high expectations of his daughter. Her life, right up until she had met the master, had seemed almost like a constant battle. She had always felt that she had to achieve so much, and do so well all of the time. So meeting the master and adopting the disciplines and belief systems must have seemed comforting, to say the least. She felt that she finally belonged and was sheltered from life in many ways. So at the time of our first meeting, the last thing the woman wanted was to make any real change and lose the relatively easy way of doing and being that having a master offered. This was despite the fact that she realized she was very miserable and stuck.

I worked with her, offering the support and strength that she needed to find and accept the master within herself, and using the techniques available to help her let go of pain from the past, especially associated with her father. When she is ready and the time is right for her, this woman will come through and will move on. But she will need to look at her pain and her fear first, before this transition can take place.

The denial and loss of connection with the whole self, including trading it for a temporary feeling of belonging and transference of personal responsibility is not necessarily the best way. It is also clearly, in my opinion, a gross neglect on the part of any master not to be aware of the individual's situation and to lead people into a belief system that dictates the focus on one specific point and one way of being, even at the cost of the wholeness of the initiate. It is important to remember that there are endless ways to go. Each reality can seem all-encompassing at certain times and spaces in our lives, but the most rewarding of all is to discover our own unique path, and to use some or all existing paths, tools and information to get there. The exciting thing is that, as we speed through our current phase of evolution, more and more people are becoming aware of the fact that they are also a master. They realize that their own crazy notions and ideas might not be so crazy after all. Indeed there are now more and more openings for individuals' perceptions of reality to be expressed and heard. This will continue to open up more and more as mankind moves forward. Nothing is only as it seems. Always expect the unexpected and remember that anything is possible. Develop your own awareness of yourself and your reality, and then you will begin to see just how amazing you are and how perfect everything really is.

Accepting differences

One of the most fascinating things for me as a clairvoyant has been the excitement and wonder that I feel when I see how each separate individual perceives reality and the different paths he or she follows to arrive at those perceptions and conclusions. No two individuals perceive in exactly the same way. This might be one of our greatest stumbling blocks, not realizing fully that we all are so very different, and yet we have a constant drive, almost need, either to fit in with others or to change others into clones of ourselves. We can learn and experience so much more when we step back and allow others as well as ourselves, to be who they really are, and accept, allow, and even expect differences between all of us.

What is happening now worldwide, I suppose, is that individuals are redeveloping their own practice of listening to others as well as listening to themselves, becoming more aware of assumptions, and delving deeper into their own feelings and thoughts. Because after all, how can we express our perception of reality to others if we do not yet have a knowledge of it ourselves? How many times do we find ourselves responding to questions about our opinions with an almost tape-recorded type of response? Are these opinions truly our own or are we simply going with the mass response? How often do we stop and realize that our opinions have changed and continue to change over time? Something we truly felt and believed in before may have changed without us even ever realizing it. Re-evaluating our perception is part of truly being the individual that we are in the here and now.

What about our children? It is often hard to say: "Well yes, you are right! I don't know why things are that way or who said they should be that way in the first place." Why don't we just take a minute to think about it? By taking this step, and being honest, perhaps we give our children one of the greatest gifts: the realization that they can choose, and have the right to accept or not to accept, speak out, bring change, and most of all, the right and the choice to think for themselves, to challenge accepted thinking and accepted belief systems, and even to challenge us, and our own thinking and beliefs.

By allowing this, we let them know that there is space and time for everyone, that we are each unique and important, and that we can and do make a difference. I believe that we also help children to overcome the blocks that we may already have, such as the idea that change and improvements are tough. We can help a generation of people realize that this is their world, that they create and decide what happens and what does not, and that they are not small and insignificant in what we call the great scheme of things. It may be time to realize that, in many ways, we do not know better than children, and much as we have to teach them, they also have to teach us.

Finally, let me point out that there are no limitations to self-healing and healing. We each have within ourselves the capacity to heal and the knowledge of how to do it. I can also see clearly that we have within us the ability to live without dying. Discovering this part of us might not be easy, but it is there and it may very well be only a matter of time in the evolution of mankind before we do not need to die. It really is possible. We have the ability within us now to choose to die or not to die, but we have not yet looked into this possibility deeply enough or located this reality within ourselves.

When we step backwards far enough, the time will come when we see that living and dying are not the beginnings and endings that we have believed and therefore made them to be. As we step back and become aware of who we truly are, we may well become intoxicated with the vastness, the greatness and the endlessness of the possibilities, realities and expressions of ourselves still waiting for us to realize. Then words such as "nothing is ever only as it seems" will fill us with excitement and a sense of adventure. Doubt and insecurities will fade into the past and we will smile as we remember how we once were.

Chapter 4

Getting Started

⤳

A wakeup call

Life does not have to mean pain. We can turn the corner of the path that mankind presently walks and choose instead to live in a state of bliss and joy. The choice is here, clearly in front of us. The time to make that choice is now. This book in essence is a wakeup call. Yes, it is time to wakeup. Are you listening? Are you really listening now? You do not have to be sick, poor or in pain. You can say today: "No more pain! Sickness, poverty and pain are no longer a part of my reality."

It often may seem hard to be who you really are. I meet many people who are afraid of being perfect, brilliant, assertive or beautiful, simply because they have faced jealousy and aggression from others in the past. And yet, there is a part within each and every one of us that wants to shine and to be recognized. All of the time that we spend hiding and standing in the shadows, we make it harder for ourselves and for others to be who we really are, to be perfect. And worse, we build more strongly the walls, barriers and confines—the imperfect—that isolate us from our real self and blissful state of being. These confines and barriers become even more solid as we accept them, and as time goes by. They often have an anesthetizing effect on us. The truth is simple: we don't need these barriers and confines, and we don't have to accept them. One small step taken by individuals can bring a huge shift for humankind.

No More Pain

When we say no more pain as individuals, we also say no more pain in our relationships, our family and our world. As long as we continue to accept pain in our reality, we perpetuate pain in our lives and our world. I challenge the idea that you cannot have one without the other. The idea that you must have light and dark, good and bad is not so, because energy, the "all that is," or whatever you prefer to call it, is without form and without expression or judgment. Anyone who has taken the time to be still or meditate, and look and feel the "all that is" will know this. The "all that is" can be whatever we choose it to be from its initial point of formlessness and nothingness.

Our conditioning, expectations, and acceptance fashion the extremes that we have previously believed to be our reality: the good and the bad, the positive and the negative. But this is a concept and a choice, the same as the concept and choice that everything can be and is perfect. We indeed have the choice to change, create and fashion our reality any way we choose. We can put aside the principles of positive, negative, black, white, light, dark, and expect and create the most and the best if we choose to do so. Do we enjoy pain? Is that why we keep it in our lives? This is a question for everyone to ask themselves, and then to look closely at their answers and to ask why they choose to keep pain in their life. The truth is, quite simply, that there are many other options, ways of doing, ways of being, and paths besides pain.

It seems we are all just a little tired—some of us are very

tired—of things being difficult. We know deep inside and are told constantly that it does not have to be that way. And yet we also receive many messages which state that nothing is worth having if it comes easily. This is all very confusing. Isn't it time to ask who decided that? Who said that things should be so difficult and that if they're not, they're not worth having? When we really look at these statements, we might even consider them ridiculous or unnecessary. Generations of individuals have lived their lives to make things easier for us. Are we so locked into our pain and the need to struggle and fight for happiness and peace, that we do not accept the happiness that is plainly in front of each one of us? We know that each day we have a choice to take anything and everything that comes our way. We can do it a hard way or in an easy and relaxed way. So how about taking the easy way and seeing "easy" as just as valuable and worthwhile as "tough," if for no other reason than doing things differently breaking an age-old pattern?

Recently, I overheard a conversation of a friend who was listening to his son's account of how his life was going. His son was feeling great; he was receiving all that he needed; one event ran smoothly into another. Then the young man asked: "But should I be expecting some difficulties now, just so I can learn how to deal with them?" The father laughed and assured his son that there was no need for this to happen, that there were many other ways to feel good about oneself and to find oneself, besides overcoming misery and difficulties. I believe he is absolutely right.

Bringing positive thinking

Choice in our lives is continuous and everywhere. Suppose you are not feeling good at this exact moment. Instead, you have a heavy, down feeling. Sometimes you don't want to deal with this feeling or dig deeper and see what this heaviness is all about right away. You would rather do that later. That's fine, but right now you want to feel great; maybe you even need to feel great. Perhaps you have an important meeting or other event coming up. Here's a simple trick to use to immediately change your reality: Be still and start repeating every positive word and feeling you can think of. For example, "I feel great. I feel brilliant. I feel happy, energized, powerful and wonderful. I feel excited and alive." Say each word as if you really mean it. Feel each word. You could continue like this: "I look great. I look beautiful. I look attractive. I look confident. I look interesting. I am powerful." After ten minutes you will have changed your mood and your own self-image and be on a higher, more positive vibration. This works. You can take action, choosing to change your reality right away at any time when you allow yourself a few moments, and decide to bring change. You can also change the atmosphere and the vibration in your environment very quickly. If you are in a room where there has just been a heated conversation, or the room makes you feel lazy, you could simply open the windows, or you could use this simple technique: Walk around the room and clap your hands two or three times in each corner. Then stand in the center of the room and clap your hands again. Now, wait a few minutes and repeat the same process. You will find that this time your clapping sounds a lot sharper and clearer. You have changed the vibration and ambience of the room by breaking up the previous vibratory pattern. You will feel the difference. There might be a sense of more openness, and a more uplifting feeling present.

On a daily basis, I suggest you include in your life this useful thought: "I am in perfect shape and perfect health." Use this thought even if it is not yet the truth. Just thinking this thought strongly once or twice a day will make a difference. By doing this you are creating that reality of perfect health. This will become even more true with the help of other parts of this book, such as finding what is right for you to eat and letting go of the past, including fear, anger and pain. Using positive affirmation and thoughts, and developing a positive self-image on a regular basis, work best together. However, each small time spent in any of these ways brings positive results on some level.

If you are ill or if the body has any kind of disease, a powerful affirmation that needs to be said every day is: "My body clears, heals and balances itself." I also recommend: "I can heal myself," "I am letting go of everything I no longer need," "I am ready for positive change," "I draw easily to myself all that I need." One of the most powerful affirmations is: "I love myself without condition."

Use these affirmations as often as you need them; develop your own positive affirmations, whatever feels right for you at the time. The idea is, initially, to get into a positive, winning frame of mind to prepare and open yourself to self-healing. "I am of pure light and pure energy," is also a very good healing affirmation. It allows you to put yourself and your physical body into a less personal, more universal mode and to recognize yourself as one with the whole, the "all that is." This in turn allows you, on a psychological level, to become open to self-healing.

Make up your mind that you are now going to be well. See yourself as well now. Visualize bright light flowing all through your body. See yourself as being whole, well and healthy. Keep going despite whatever physical factors are standing in your way. Let yourself really believe and know that anything is possible, don't just hope that things will work. Remember that any time a negative thought comes to you, look into it deeper and ask yourself, "Where is this thought coming from?" Don't give up. Keep asking questions because you do have the answers. It may take days or even longer to find the answers, but they will come because they are within yourself.

Positive thoughts and affirmations are now used daily by many people. But positive thinking still isn't understood or explored enough yet for real magic and lasting positive change to be enjoyed by everyone rather than just a few. It is a relatively new pathway, and there is a lot that must be taken into account in order for this process to work. Sheer will power and the desire for health, peace and happiness is a start, but not enough to bring that reality to ourselves collectively at this time. We still have many fixed boundaries within our consciousness and awareness. Anything is possible but we need first to discover, examine, and let go of all within us that says it is not.

Sometimes we hold on to a particular affliction. For example, it could be a skin rash that keeps reappearing; perhaps it is an ulcer in the mouth; or a swollen hand that never quite gets better. There was a man in my case studies who suffered from a constant headache for years. Sometimes, people hold onto a particular problem for a reason. The reason can be that you feel the need for a barometer in your life to let you know and feel that you are really here, really present, alive and taking part in life, a reminder that you are real and so is everything around you. At times, people need to have this grounding feeling. Pain and ailments can be used in this way. It could also be that you only get this particular problem when you are tired and overdoing things, not taking care of or making time for yourself, or that your life is not working in any number of other ways. Be aware and check out this possibility. If you do see and feel that you are holding on to ailments, know that you also have the choice to say that you no longer wish to use pain in this way. Initially, after making this decision, you may need to find another barometer, a non-physical painless one, to let you know where and how you are within yourself at any given time.

Pain and punishment

The herpes virus is an interesting case of pain and punishment. Although it is believed to be incurable, there is a way to manage it with or without the use of medication: a change in lifestyle, a reduction of stress and a knowledge of how to deal with stress in positive ways. A healthy balanced diet is also strongly recommended for this particular condition. When the body becomes stressed and out of balance and the diet is inadequate, an outbreak of the virus reappears. Interestingly, Herpes is also accepted to be linked to the nervous system.

Some time ago, I had a client with this condition. She was a very loving, nurturing young woman who had been through an abusive childhood into her teens. Some people would have judged her as promiscuous, but she really enjoyed the intimacy and attention that an active sex life brought her. She was religious and had some guilt about her sexual activities with varied partners. She recalls a particular time when she felt that if she made love with a particular man, it would turn out badly and that she would be punished. She felt guilty about her deep attraction and desire for this person. She went ahead anyway and made love with him. She also slept with two other men before her first outbreak appeared. She was subsequently diagnosed with the herpes virus. She is not sure, even now, which one of those men transmitted the virus to her. In fact, she realizes that she might have been carrying the virus long before the outbreak. Looking back, she realized, however, how low her self-esteem was at that time, how guilty she felt about sex, and how much she felt that she deserved to be punished. She also realized that the thought of something bad happening was very powerful for her, one that could even have brought about the manifestation of the virus. Many times we create negative situations in our life because we feel bad about ourselves and deep down we feel we deserve to be punished. This is a strong reason to have positive feelings and opinions about yourself at all times.

This case is a good illustration of getting what you

expect and what you feel you deserve. On the positive side, if you expect the best, you will get the best as you clear and heal yourself. With practice of positive thoughts and with the passage of time, you will receive the best and not be disappointed. So stay with positive thinking. It works and it is simple. However, if positive thinking has not worked for you in the past, you need to look into yourself a little more deeply.

It's always good and often necessary to look into ourselves and our lives a little more deeply. Being accident-prone is clearly another instance of pain self-allowed even if it might not seem so. Steven L. Dubovsky M.D. says in his book *Mind Body* that there is a range of individuals who hurt themselves. It could be self-inflicted injuries or self-mutilation, people carving their skin, cutting themselves, hitting themselves or starving their body. It's quite plain that these people have a problem generally rooted in the past, associated with natural human emotions and needs that wish to be expressed such as shame, fear, guilt, anger, anxiety, grief, love, dependency or sexual longings. Dubovsky refers to psychoanalyst Flanders-Dunbar who observed that self-destructive behavior is one way to transfer intolerable mental conflict about others into the bodily realm. There are also individuals who, without any conscious intention, repeatedly accidentally hurt themselves. We will all recognize the accident-prone syndrome in ourselves even in very small ways.

The more I looked into this accident-prone syndrome, the more I realized the truth of these theories, which goes with my belief and understanding that there are no mistakes or accidents. We do all know exactly what we are doing, even though it may not be so on a conscious level or apparent to us at all times. So the next time you fall or stub your toe, or have a more serious kind of accident, do not write the incident off. Just take a moment to look at what is really going on in your life in the immediate or even distant past. Why would you allow yourself to be hurt in this way? How many times have you had what you might consider a "bad" thought and then hurt yourself almost immediately afterwards?

A short while ago, one of my clients decided to end a relationship that had become intolerable to her. Her husband had been having an affair for five years. He refused to give up his mistress and spent half the week with her and the other half with his wife. My client had tried everything to change the situation. On three separate occasions, consumed by anger, frustration and pain, she had gone out to the other woman's house to see if indeed her husband's car was parked outside his mistress' door. On these three separate occasions she had had minor car accidents, but nothing very serious had happened to her physically. It was almost as if the car became an extension of herself and she would run it into the curve as if to vent some of her built-up frustration. Each time she was shocked at what happened, not realizing that she was the one creating this reality.

Finally, one evening, she had jumped into her car and sped to the bank intending to empty their joint account and leave. She did not make it. Instead she crashed the car on the freeway and was badly hurt. This woman had to be cut out of her vehicle. The car was wrecked. After a stay in the hospital, she returned home to re-consider her position and to think again how to proceed. She clearly saw how her emotions that night led to the accident and how dangerous those emotions had become. For this woman, the accidents that she kept creating were a strong wake-up call, a reminder that she needed to step back outside of her emotions.

If you are constantly hurting yourself or being what you consider "accident-prone," it is time to look more deeply at yourself and your life, because your body and your mind are ready to tell you so much more about yourself—where you are and how you feel—than you might have previously imagined.

Self-belief

What makes us doubt ourselves and our self-healing abilities? Some people have doubts because of all the people around them who tell them to believe in others, rather than themselves. Others doubt because of all the small hurts, pains and disappointments that have accumulated throughout the years. Ask yourself where your doubts are coming from. You will need to look and deal with everything in your life that says you cannot practice self-healing or that it probably will not work. Sometimes the feeling and little voices of negativity and doubt within you will be loud, clear and easy to deal with. At other times, the doubts and fears may be subtle and not so easy to pinpoint. But there is an end to the process, so keep going. Remember, regardless of how it may seem, you do have the answers. How could you not? You are already "all that is," with access to all questions and answers. These may seem like empty words, but they form a truth and reality within us all.

I recently worked with a man who was hospitalized in another state far away from my home. His son contacted me and was desperate. His father was on a ventilator and one of his lungs had collapsed. I agreed to work with him remotely until a good healer could be found in the family's area. I received a picture of the man and his name through the mail. I tuned into him and realized that he was in bad condition. The first thing I saw was that this man needed fluid drained from his lungs. I worked on this on a spiritual and healing level. The next day, the hospital carried out this step and drained the lungs. I realized the man was afraid and did not believe that he could breathe alone. I worked with him by building up his confidence and belief in himself and asked his son and wife to do the same during their daily visits.

During the self-healing process, it is important to realize how much belief exists in you the individual, or anyone else you may be helping to heal. Sometimes you may feel that you want to be well, that you have total belief in being well, and that you are following all the requirements necessary for healing to work, but you are not making the progress you want. In such a case, ask yourself how much you really believe in what you are doing, and what your blocks are. Blocks and non-beliefs will make themselves known at some point. Often people are surprised at finding their own blocks despite their belief that they were totally open to the process.

In this man's case, I worked for another two days, helping him to believe in himself. Twice, the medical staff tried to take him off the ventilator but with no success. I kept going and told his son to get his father to visualize that he was breathing by himself, and to go through the motions of breathing even though he was not actually breathing alone. This finally worked and the patient was taken off the ventilator. The patient's belief in what he could do and his conquest of his fear were paramount in his success.

Even those of us who have had what we consider a perfect childhood and a relatively happy life have doubts, fears and mental or emotional blocks on some level, even if we don't recognize them. For others who have had difficult lives, these negatives are increased. For example, you might have moved and had to go to a new school. Perhaps you were popular and confident before the move, and then suddenly everything was gone. You felt very alone and insecure in your new school, and could not understand why people did not seem to like you. Perhaps a new brother or sister came along. You no longer felt secure in your family placement. Being told that you are stupid, not good enough or bad in any way, being beaten or abused on the emotional, physical or mental level, all take their toll on our self-belief.

Many years ago I had a childhood friend who told me the following story. Judith, seven years old, was put to bed at a reasonable hour even though it was vacation time. She slept in a comfortable bed with crisp white sheets and a solid polished wooden headboard. Judith had an active mind and was not tired or ready to go to sleep, but she was afraid to get out of bed, as her mother was very strict, and might catch her. Then she would be in trouble. Playing with her hair, Judith discovered a hairpin that had been forgotten despite her bedtime wash and brush routine. She took the hairpin out of her hair, chewed off the plastic end covering and proceeded to draw on the polished surface of the headboard of the bed. She was lost in her imagination and in no time at all had covered the entire surface with pictures, patterns, symbols and shapes, scratching deeply into the wood. Finally she fell asleep. The next morning, discovering the damage to the headboard, Judith's mother pulled the small girl roughly out of the bed and exploded with rage. The mother was beside herself with anger and disbelief. The little girl went without food for most of the day and was confined to the house. Her mother promised Judith that she would be deeply sorry for what she had done and threatened all kind of horrible things. The main threat was "wait until your father gets home." That night, when her father did get home, the mother cried, raged and called the girl "an ungrateful wretch," "an animal not decent to live with nice people and nice things." The father was tired from a hard day's work and felt compelled to do something drastic to appease his wife's rage. He took his leather belt and went upstairs to the bedroom where Judith was lying in bed very afraid. Without a word he pulled back the covers and proceeded to beat the little girl on her back and bare bottom, leaving red marks. He was not a sadistic man by nature, so the beating was not too harsh. After it was over Judith cried herself to sleep. Her heart felt as if it was breaking as she stifled her sobs with the pillow.

The pain in her chest was unbearable. She had never before felt so alone.

Judith did not understand exactly what she had done that was so very wrong. Children often don't realize the value that adults give to objects that surround them. Yet she felt that she must be very bad and worthless for her father to use a belt on her, as he never had done so before and never did again. The red marks on her body faded after a few days, but the marks left in her heart and in her mind stayed with her for a long time. It took years for Judith to express herself openly and artistically again.

Hopefully, children are no longer treated in these ways today. Rules are not as strict, and the needs and behavior of both children and parents are more understood. Today, Judith might have been given a book to read before she went to sleep or pencils and paper to use. In the past, children were often treated cruelly and brutally in the home and in school, and then left with little or no knowledge of how to heal those deep emotional scars they carried with them into their adult lives.

There is no point in bringing blame for what we might have suffered at the hands of others in the past as children, but it is important to know that we can heal these emotional wounds as well as the physical ones. We can all move on and find happiness. But remember, even if you feel that you have had a perfect life, it's the small things that you may not even think affected you that really do leave their mark. These need to be healed and cleared. Regression therapy can be immensely helpful in dealing with past traumas.

Some of the many ways to heal your self-belief are mentioned throughout this book. But in order to find and build self-belief again you will need to keep going, keep questioning and becoming aware of yourself. Remember also, these negative thought patterns about yourself do not only come from the past, but are developed often without awareness day by day. So be aware of your thoughts, because they are as real and solid as you are. I clearly remember some years ago, everything in my life was going great. I was on top of the world, feeling happy and having an absolutely perfect day. Just for a brief moment I thought: "It's almost too good to be true." Within hours, there was chaos; everything came crashing down around me and took days to put back together. I smile now when I remember that day; it was a good lesson for me to be aware of what one single thought can do.

Facing your fears

Fear is one of the biggest obstacles in the self-healing process. You are going to have to face your fears: fear of your particular disease or imbalance; fear of a part of your body no longer working. For example, if you have growths and tumors that you can physically see and feel, or any other imbalance that manifests physically, realize that if you are disgusted with these parts of your body, you also isolate yourself from them. They are, for the time being, a part of you, so you are going to need to conquer your fear of their presence. The same applies to AIDS, herpes, or anything that has to do with the so-called abnormal cells and viruses. I watch many people with these conditions wage a battle with affected parts of their body. They visualize blasting these areas with bright light or energy, using a lot of energy and willpower in the process. They often come away frustrated because there is no change. Yes, it is very important to be focused on your specific out-of-balance area. But check that your aggressive blasting of these parts is not simply masking your fear—a fear of feeling deep down that you might not make it, that the unwanted imbalance will not leave, or that you don't have the strength or knowledge to heal yourself.

These are two ways you might work. I suggest a combination of both. First, focus on healing thoughts, color, light and energy on specific body areas that need help. Second, flood the complete body with healing light, color, and energy. Each time you have an opportunity to be outside, and to be still, take it. To be still and to be in the "all that is" can be felt in many different ways: a quietness, a peace and calm coming from deep inside of you as you breathe and let everything go; a feeling of loving and enjoying the moment to the point that it feels as if there exists no past or future, only a moment in time and space where your heart center opens and you feel warm all over loving yourself, everything and everybody else unconditionally in that moment. Perhaps you also know deep down inside of you that nothing really matters and everything will be all right, that everything in this moment and beyond is exactly as it needs to be. All of these feelings bring with them a feeling of strength, calm and control, a pleasant reminder of all the strength that you really have. Be in this "quiet" and the space of "all that is." Enjoy the vastness of everything around you. Let yourself go and be a part of it. Merge with it. Draw it all into yourself and have the thought that you are taking and filling yourself with all that you need. If you cannot physically be outside, do not allow that to be a barrier. Decide that walls are not going to stop you. Visualize yourself expanding through the entire room; let yourself become bigger than the room, bigger than the building, the street, the area, the country, or the world. Reach far into the universe, letting go of everything you don't need with each outward breath, and taking in all that you need with each inward breath. Using your mind, you can also imagine that you are sitting in a great, big, beautiful garden on a warm sunny day, or a desert island, with waves gently lapping at your feet, or any other place that makes you feel rested and good.

For people who are seriously ill or have been ill for a long time, there is a path back to health too. Whatever positive affirmation and thought you have, whatever healing visualization you use, whatever you commit within yourself to taking control of your own healing process, is good and valuable. It will bring positive change on some level. The point is that you can do something with thought no matter how ill you are. If there is much pain present initially, you will probably already be receiving medication. This may be necessary because, although there will be some people who can focus despite pain, it can be a barrier for others. So continue to be realistic by accepting the help you need until you reach the point where you no longer need help for pain. In short, if you are in great pain, it is all right to seek help via medication or other treatments, the same as if you are in an accident or life-threatening situation. Of course then, you will need to accept any and all help available. So work with what is available and use self-healing to enhance the healing process, but be flexible. Also, be prepared to feel pain sometimes and don't let your fear stop you; be assured that it does have an end. Let pain wash over you at least once. It will then lose much of its fearful aspect, and you will no longer feel it in the same way. Feel and understand pain and then let it go, for you will no longer have any need for it.

Living and dying

There are many good books on the subject of death and dying. There are cultures where death is not mourned or seen as an end, but rather a beginning. In our time, death is a subject that needs to be further explored. The fear factor must be taken out because as long as we fear death, we still fear life. Pioneers such as Elizabeth Kubler-Ross, among others, have helped bring the subject of death out into the open and much good work is being done. A book I read years ago and recommend is *The Tibetan Book of the Dead*, because it shows us a different perspective from a different culture. The Mayan culture also brings another perspective on death. The Mayan people believed that one of the important steps of a mortal's spiritual transcendence was to look into the individuals' fated future death, face that future death scenario, realize that it could be changed, and then change it.

A couple of years ago, I filmed fifty volunteers who wanted to see and experience for themselves the end of their present lives, to visit their own death scenarios, to die and see what death and beyond was like for them. Progression therapy was used for this experience. The volunteers moved forward in time and experienced the end of their lives, death and beyond. The results were interesting and varied. A handful of the volunteers afterwards decided that they would then change their future death scenarios. They each had their own reasons for doing this. One overweight man saw that he was going to die from a heart attack much sooner than he had expected, leaving behind a wife and a small son. The man vowed to change his lifestyle from that day on. A woman saw herself dying alone and afraid, estranged from her family and loved ones because of bitterness and misunderstandings that had built up throughout her life. She too decided that this was not the ending that she wanted and she committed herself to change.

Simply with awareness, changing your death as well as your life can be done easily. You only need to look ahead and then make the decision, followed by whatever changes are necessary. Then, if you decide that death will continue to be part of your reality, you create a different future death reality.

One of the best possible things that you can do for a friend or loved one who is very ill or dying is to visualize them being flooded by bright yellow, gold, blue, purple or white light inside and outside of their body. If someone is dying, you can make their passing easier by helping them to let go and by working on your own "letting go" issues. Many people are very afraid of death and loss. Some try to hide their anger, pain and despair from their dying loved ones. There are often cases where the person may not be told that they are dying and every one tries to act normally, denying what is happening. This is a very personal decision of course, but bear in mind that although those who take part in this facade may feel they are protecting the loved one, in fact, they are stopping the loved one from consciously facing what we, as a society, have accepted as the natural process of death, and preparing for that transition.

The Tibetan Book of the Dead shows how another culture spends a lifetime preparing for that "death transition." I am not suggesting that this is good or bad, but it is worth looking at as another perspective.

As parents, we wish to shield our children from pain. But the wise parent will be there for the child and help the child deal with painful situations in his or her own way, realizing that pain is at present, an accepted part of life's experiences. So with "dying", bring light, love and support and deal with your own issues as they occur within the experience you are involved in. When I refer to dying in this way I am speaking of people who are, without doubt, at the end of their lives and somewhere within themselves have accepted the reality that they must die. At this point, even if the impending death appears to be sudden or unexpected, if you look really closely and objectively, you will realize that signs had already been there for some time.

We must look then even more closely at ourselves and others and begin to truly realize and accept that we know more about what we are doing and creating than we ever before imagined.

Wants and needs

Some of us realize that what we want and what we need can be two very different things. Many times we want things, not because we need them but because we want or need to know that we can have them. A simple way towards clearly defining your wants and needs is to make a list of them, both in the long and short term. Deny yourself nothing, because anything is possible. At the same time, go into yourself more deeply, really ask yourself which particular person and part of yourself has these wants and needs. For example, most people at some point want to be rich or famous. If this is you, ask yourself why and be honest about the answers. Do you feel that this desire is coming from the past? Or is it coming from the present, due to a lack of recognition in your life or a lack of material possessions? Now ask yourself again: does the child in you want or need this? Does the adolescent want or need these things or is it the adult you? Ask the different parts of yourself. It is possible you will be surprised at your own answers.

Getting what you want and need and realizing how much you really want or need is often measured by the level of commitment or centeredness you will have to use to create the reality. As we go through life, often our wants and needs are fulfilled in unexpected ways or in smaller ways. If you find yourself being fulfilled without getting exactly what you felt you desired in the first place, feel good about it. It does not mean that you gave up or could not make it to the end of the line. Perhaps you saw other things that you accepted as more important along the way. Compromise is always acceptable if it is thought through and truly accepted within ourselves. If not, it causes chaos, misery and suppression, a recipe for illness and imbalance. One of the most exciting things about life is the way we realize, as time passes, that our initial wants and needs which had once seemed so big are often obtained in even bigger ways than we had originally desired, or even thought about. The next time things do not work out as you want them to, tell yourself that there is something better for you. You will be amazed how fast and how often this turns out to be true.

If there are needs which remain unfulfilled in your life, and if you give up on the hope of meeting those needs, pretending to yourself that they don't really matter, you are in a state of deep denial and emotional despair. Then, even all the good and great things that you do have or feel are overshadowed by this down feeling, lurking in the background of your mind, emotions and being.

It's important then to be honest with yourself. The inability to let go of the past, of people or lifestyles or ways of being can also be a cause of depression. This often leads you to not feeling good enough. You reason, how can I be such a free and powerful being and yet not have what I need from life or not be able to let go of the past? We often deal with depression by using antidepressants. Although certain people feel that antidepressants are useful in times of great struggle, stress, and emotional overload, they should be seen as a brief interlude. They may give a person time to build themselves up to the point where they feel ready to look at their situation and then take some form of action regarding the initial causes of the depression. When antidepressants are taken long-term, they tend to serve as a blanket, which may further suppress the initial emotions to the point that it is difficult to reconnect with them. Medication, therefore, might not be the best answer. It is always advisable to seek the advice of your physician before coming off antidepressants or any other medication and to be aware of what the effects of this action will be in both physical and non-physical terms.

A long time ago, I knew a man who was obsessed with making money. While he was making money, he was great. But at the first sign of his business going downhill or facing financial collapse, he would have a nervous breakdown. This had happened several times throughout his life. He was diagnosed as manic-depressive. There was a general pattern to his breakdowns. He would begin behaving in strange ways. Spending huge amounts of money on things he did not need. Giving gifts to strangers. Spending many days not sleeping and being very hyperactive. When this happened, he would be committed to an institution by his relatives, and sedated. Often lithium was administered along with other medications. After a varying amount of time, anywhere from a few days up to a month, he would be released and start to build his life all over again. Doctors told him that he had a chemical imbalance in his brain and that he needed to take medication all of his life to stay in balance.

Finally, this man broke the pattern. He met a woman and got into a healthy relationship. When he started to have a breakdown, the woman called his relatives and the authorities. She told them that although he was having what looked like the usual breakdown and imbalance, this time he was not going to go to the institution or take medication. Instead, she took him to a quiet peaceful place. And with the support of a therapist, she helped him not only release and work through his past pain, but also to see that he was not judged by the amount of money he made. Over time, she also helped him to find the amazing person within himself that he really was.

The man saw that at the times of the breakdowns in his life, he needed a quiet and peaceful place to work things through. He also needed support and understanding. He came through that time and has never looked back. Basically, he decided to challenge the patterns that he was creating and also the accepted remedies to those patterns. He also challenged what he had previously allowed, which was the belief that other people knew what was right for him. He had finally found another human being to tell him that he could work it out himself, someone who offered him solid support.

I'm not suggesting that everyone who has been diagnosed

as manic-depressive should take this same action. But as this case shows, it can be done, and therefore, it's something to think about if another individual is going through a similar situation. We often know more about our own mind and how it works than others do. We have lived with our mind for a long time and we truly do not need to "fit into" or accept textbook descriptions of how our mind works.

Fitting in is a choice. There may come a time for each of us when we see that fitting in is not necessarily the best choice for us, maybe because it does not truly give us what we need to find fulfillment and happiness. In taking that step forward and really looking at ourselves, we may also open new pathways for others to follow along the journey of discovery, ending with us embracing our uniqueness and further expanding the rich and colorful tapestry of life's endless possibilities, the untold realizations just waiting to be found. Finally, we stretch ourselves beyond concepts and limitations and realize they are not truly ours.

The perfect you

You will need to explore what "being perfect" means to you. Realistically, the perfect you and the perfect somebody else could be very different. For instance, if you have feet you consider too big, a nose too long or a voice too high, you may need to love and accept these parts of yourself just as they are. Instead of dwelling on those parts, shift your focus from what you consider imperfect, as there are so many other things to do and to be. The thought "I love myself completely without condition" works well at these times. There is no point comparing yourself to others, because whether you can see it now or not, you are absolutely perfect just as you are. When you compare yourself to anyone, you create mental and emotional blocks within yourself. There are endless reasons why you chose to be as you are in the first place. You may have forgotten these reasons, but they can be rediscovered if you decide to start looking. If you really feel dissatisfied with yourself and your life, start digging deep within yourself and find out why you chose this particular body, this particular look, this particular state of health. Why did you choose this particular way to be? And remember, don't stop, keep looking because you do have the answers.

Personally, I spent many years not being comfortable with my body, feeling I did not have complete control over how it looked in the ways that other people seemed to. The body parts did not all seem to go together somehow. It was as if I had the arms of one person, the face and the head of another and so on. After a long time, I realized that I was quite lucky to be aware of these differences and that all of these different parts could mold and mesh together. I felt comfortable and accepting of them. Furthermore, I realized that, from within, I could have my body shining like the very brightest star, and could attract constant attention, or I could also fade into nothingness and never be noticed. The choice was mine, and as I accepted that fact, my body did more and more meshing and molding and flowing together to become one.

Of course, there are endless ways that you can look at the body images that you portray. There are those that you copy from others, or that you create as if for the very first time. Have fun with these images. As you accept yourself, the "perfect you" can and will be expanded to people around you, outside of you and within you. The changes may not be all apparent in one day but will happen and become noticeable to varying degrees as time goes by.

If you really want to bring change to others, bring it to yourself first, because others are a reflection of you. If you want to do a little more, think of those you want to help and imagine them in a wide-open, empty space filled and surrounded by bright yellow, blue, lilac or white light. Just by doing this you will give these people all the room and all the light that they need to bring positive change into their lives. This works even for those people who are most difficult to be around.

For the moment, doing this for others is enough. Right now, concentrate on yourself first. It is important because during the self-healing process, we need to put ourselves first. Many of us have forgotten how to do this, hoping that if we heal others, we will also heal ourselves. This does work as well, but initially put yourself first. Work on yourself until you have wellness and balance.

One of the most powerful affirmations that I have experienced is: "I am perfect." If you keep giving this message to yourself, you allow yourself to be perfect as you are, and all that in your eyes was not perfect falls away. For many people, to say "I am perfect" does not come easily for a variety of reasons. We have been conditioned to believe in modesty, to feel that, in using such an affirmation, we are being egocentric, a state of being identified some time ago by psychiatrists and psychoanalysts. It's become a negative term, with connotations of selfishness, another state of being that we also have come to believe is bad.

If saying "I am perfect" is hard to accept, I suggest you begin by having for a few days the thought in your mind and using verbally the affirmation: "I love myself completely without condition." When you do this, you open yourself to self-love and self-belief, and allow yourself to shift to another reality and vibration, moving away from false modesty and from the sense of keeping yourself down and having all kinds of problems, pains, illnesses and dramas. When you accept the "I am perfect" affirmation and realization, the realities and joy that you create and bring to your life will feel much smoother and make more sense than the chaos you have previously lived with all the time that you were seeing yourself as flawed. When you say clearly "I am perfect," you bring to yourself a deep sense of the profound, and the feeling and expression of much self-love. This affirmation is a most healing one and those who do it often feel a great relief. For someone who has spent a lifetime feeling bad, not good enough, and carrying emotional pain, this affirmation can be a life-changing, even life-saving, shift. Remember, "I am perfect" is a truth and a reality. It is a choice for you to make. When you realize and accept perfection in yourself, you open an even greater doorway to yourself, the universe and the "all that is."

Self-healing is a possibility for us all. It is a choice for each of us to make. The degree that we use it in our lives will differ. The more we see that self-healing works, the more confident we will become with our own abilities and the more we will rely on ourselves. Start by saying no to pain and punishment. Face your fears, bring positive thinking and joy to every moment of your life, love your body without condition, and always remember that you are a perfect and wonderful being.

Remember too that despite how anything may look, you do know what you are doing and you do not make mistakes. It has not been a mistake to bring illness into your life. It will not be a mistake to bring health.

Chapter 5

Color, Crystals and Touch

～

Color

Color is everywhere, both in and out of our lives and beyond our believed reality. It has been realized by many that we are made up of vibrations, and vibrations are colors. A person who is aware and attuned, perhaps a sensitive or clairvoyant, someone who has developed and allowed their ability to see clearly, will often see persons and objects giving off and being surrounded by colors. These colors are termed as auras and energy fields. These beliefs may also be concepts which we still do not yet understand enough, but on some level they do exist and work.

Although we live in a very colorful world, it is interesting how many people in so much of our world still live and dress in black and white or dark, muted colors like gray, brown, dark blue, green and burgundy. Yet on the other hand, many so-called primitive people enjoy and live with much more color than the so-called developed parts of our world. Society generally goes along with fashion trends, and people accept that in autumn and winter dark colors should be worn. This is strange when you think that the skies and the weather in these seasons are often dark and do nothing much to give you a lift when you need one. It's almost as if by wearing these dark colors, we blend in with the dreariness of these times of the year. Sadly, many people only allow themselves to enjoy bright warm colors such as orange, yellow, lime green, blue, lilac, pink and purple during the warmer seasons or for very special events. Yet many people have been surprised to find themselves feeling especially good when they wear and surround themselves with bright and beautiful colors. The good news is that fashion seems to be changing in Europe and this change is spreading to the United States. As I write, color is in fashion, and yellow, pink and blue are at the top of the list, while last year it was purple. Even presenters on television are beginning to be seen more often in vibrant colors.

There are some common misunderstandings associated with particular colors. For instance, the color black has often been feared. It has been believed to represent the unknown. Black in the past and even now has had associations of somehow being bad. But if you put aside your own preconceived ideas and fears, you will see that black has depth, that you can look into the color black and use it as a doorway to forever.

Many healers also have a fixed belief system about color. They state that specific colors are needed for specific areas of healing. For example, blue is accepted for calming, yellow for intellectual openness and mental clarity, white for purity, and purple for power. However, these beliefs can also be based on associations that may or may not be valid. I say that colors do not need to be fixed or used only in these ways. I strongly suggest that you find out what works for you by exploring every color, not only the ones that you like. Check out the ones you don't like and realize for yourself why you don't like them. We will, of course, all have our personal favorites. I love purple, yellow, orange, pink, lime green, and white.

If you feel that you have a difficult time visualizing color, try this: Gather a collection of colors, pieces of card, or perhaps cloth. Try the basic bold colors first and then go on to pastels. Practice sitting with each color, one at a time. Have the color in front of you and look at it for a while. Feel its own individual vibration. Get used to that particular feeling. How does it make you feel? Make a note of this, then close your eyes and continue to see it in your mind. Remember that it's not necessary to see the color in vivid details in your mind; just the basic outline and feeling, even using the name of the color is enough. Keep practicing. Be patient. After a while, you will find that you can visualize color instantly. To explore each color, simply make a list of at least eight to ten basic colors. For example: red, yellow, blue, green, orange, black, white and purple. Picture each color and when you have finished writing them down, feel them one by one. Allow yourself the enjoyment of imagining that you are being totally surrounded by beautiful, exquisite color and light. Imagine that you are bathing and floating in warm colors and energies. Take deep breaths through your mouth from the bottom of your stomach and feed yourself with these warm colors and energies. See how each different one feels and how it affects you. What does each color bring to you? Make a note of each thought, feeling, emotion and association. If you are working with yellow and you think about and feel the sun, this is an association, so don't stop there. Ask yourself: "What else do I feel? What else does yellow bring to me?" and keep going with this process. Yellow might also make you feel warm, joyful, light-headed or even cold. Notice exactly what this color does for you, but concentrate on your feelings, pictures and emotions rather than intellectual association. By exploring color in this way, you will find not only what works for you, but your own unique links with these specific vibrations, and you will discover how to use them. Colors are unlimited building materials of non-physical matter which we all use in the creating of our reality and in the healing process.

For those who meditate or who have noticed, during times when they are between waking and sleep, the very different colors and shapes that also exist but do not seem to be a part of this world, I would say enjoy these other shades and colors. Enjoy the diversity. Use them. Experience them and explore them as you would colors and shades that you are familiar with because, of course, they are just as real and useful. I would also advise taking the experience a step further. Stay with these other more unusual colors you see or feel for a while and experience the places and spaces where they exist and are coming from. In doing so, even for a moment, you expand your own awareness and allow one more barrier and limitation to fall away. Mentally, it might be helpful to imagine these colors in lines. Follow the lines. Trace the sources. Have fun and enjoy the wonder and exploration of color.

A while ago, I was on a flight back home from Arizona. I was seated next to a cheerful elderly lady. We began talking and she proudly announced that she was 81 years old. I told her that she looked great, as indeed, she did. This lady went on to explain her secrets for looking and feeling good. She said that for the past ten years, she never watched any negative news on television, but only accepted the positives in her life, and she always wore bright, cheerful colors. She said that once she had reached the age of 70—an age she had never imagined she would see—she decided to make the most of life and enjoy every single moment, and indeed she was doing just that. I thought this was great, but also just a little ironic that it had taken this cheerful lady 70 years to reach the conclusion to wear color and only accept positives into her reality. But it also shows us that it's never too late to change our perception and ways of doing things. Indeed, I have worked with individuals in their seventies and eighties who wanted to change their lives and experience a rebirthing session. Maybe it's time to look in your closet now and bring color into your life and remember that someone has to start somewhere. You might be surprised at how many of your friends and family will admire you for bringing color into your life and wardrobe. Who knows? You could start your own fashion statement and trends. Dare to be different, dare to be yourself! Dare to feel good!

Color can also be expanded into many other areas of your life, such as the food you eat, and the way you decorate your environment. Merely choose what feels good and enjoy. Your preferences may change as time goes by, but for now, the "now" is important and so are you, so make choices. I have lost count of the times people have visited my very colorful home and loved it, but said: "I have always wanted to do this, but it might be difficult when we resell the house." Or they say: "I would love to paint my house with bright colors but I am only going to be there for six months." The answer is clear. Make things as you want them to be, now. You can always change them back later if you need to. And remember that six months isn't only six months. It's six months of your life! It is important and you can feel good in it now, so why deprive yourself? Don't wait for the future. Allow yourself color in your life now.

There are different ways to use color in self-healing. Begin to think of color as material which is needed to feed, soothe, enhance and heal you and your life. During a healing session, you can visualize and direct a color to a particular part of your body; you can surround yourself by color and you can fill all of your body with color. You can also use different colors during the same session.

How can you become more in tune to color? Start thinking in color more often. You can start by simply asking yourself what color or colors the new person that you just met is "being." Or as you are talking to someone who you have known for ages, just ask: "What color is this person 'being' at this moment?" Believe in your own feelings. Apply color to relationships, events, countries and the entire world. Use it in all different kinds of ways. Thinking in color is a major mental first step, which leads to actually seeing people in color, with energy fields and auras. The more you practice, the more it will become second nature to you.

We will see in chapter 9 how to apply color in self-healing. For now, I suggest two simple exercises. First, relax and surround yourself with color using your mind, and breathe it from the bottom of your stomach all through your body. The second exercise is to surround yourself and breathe color through your body. Then expand yourself within that color all the way out from your body, expanding and covering the room. Have the color you are surrounded with expand with you. Let go of everything you do not need just by having that thought in mind. On the way back, when you return into yourself and the color gets smaller and smaller around you, remember that you are gathering everything that you need just by having the following thought: "I am easily gathering all that I need." Remember that color is very real. When you feel tired or down, just take a moment and ask yourself: "What color do I need right now?" Go with your feeling. Imagine that color and breathe it through your body. By doing this, you are replenishing yourself. Even a few breaths of color will give you what you need.

Bring color into your life and experience the wonderfully positive benefits of color for yourself, because we are all colorful people whether we realize this yet or not.

Crystals

Crystals, like color, can be a useful element in your self-healing process. You can heal without them, but they can be comforting and enjoyable, magnifying your own energies, positive thoughts and self-healing techniques. While they are not necessary, they can be viewed as a useful healing companion. Let's look at a few of the different types of crystals available and their recommended uses.

I recommend that you obtain crystals in their natural state, whenever possible, unpolished. You may have a crystal store in your area. You might find crystals at New Age stores or perhaps at a healing center. If you live somewhere in the world where you can go and mine your own crystals, this can be a lot of fun too. It is an exciting experience to go to a crystal mine and sift through the loads of earth that have been brought up to the surface from the open mines and to unearth your very own crystals. Lots of crystal mines are privately owned and invite the public to do just that for a small fee. Arkansas has been a great place for me to go and gather crystals. Of course, the nearer you get to places where crystals are found in abundance the lower the price will be that you pay for them. With quartz crystal, for instance, it is possible to pay very reasonable prices for quite large pieces. The clearer and more transparent the piece, the more expensive it will be. I do not believe that clearer quality necessarily makes for a more powerful crystal.

Different stones are believed and accepted to have different associations, qualities and behaviors. The clear quartz crystal has various names such as witches mirror, star stone, and zaztun. Quartz is credited with many uses, which include protection, healing, development and enhancement of psychic powers and other calming and soothing effects.

Another favorite for many is the beautiful purple amethyst. This crystal can be easily found and it is credited with powers such as enhanced dreams, healing, peace, love, and development of psychic abilities. Amethyst is a very popular crystal loved and used by many. Personally, I recommend placing a piece of this crystal under your pillow to promote deep peaceful sleep and prophetic dreams, also to help you find and connect with the answers you need during your self-healing process.

Rose quartz is another crystal that is found in abundance. It is generally a very pale pink, although it can be much darker. Rose quartz is generally credited as being a particularly healing and nurturing crystal. If you feel emotionally stressed or drained, try this short exercise: Place the Rose quartz crystal flat on your stomach next to your skin. After a while you will feel it becoming warm; you'll start to be aware of its loving soothing vibration. Just a few minutes of holding it on the stomach area will make you feel relaxed, soothed, and energized. Rose quartz is a great soother, calmer and balancer. It is especially useful when you feel that you are giving so much to others and not receiving enough in return for yourself.

You might try placing different crystals on your chosen focus points of your body while you lie flat or fall asleep with them. One of my personal favorite crystals is Lapis Lazulis. This stone has been recognized since ancient times as bringing wisdom and helping to develop psychic abilities. In India, it is given to children to wear threaded, often on gold thread, as a form of protection. Lapis Lazulis in an unpolished form can be rather expensive and difficult to obtain. You could buy a polished piece and then have it sliced through to obtain a flat slice. This flat slice is perfect to use during meditation. Place it flat on your forehead. Feel the weight of the piece. See the dark outline of its shape. You may see a lighter color on the inside of the outline. Initially, just doing this is enough. After a couple of sessions, imagine that you are looking with the mind's eye through the piece of Lapis while your eyes remain closed. You may see a few speckles of light, a glow or perhaps a white tunnel. Always follow tunnels through to see where they are going. There are many possible places they will take you. Try this exercise perhaps twice a week for not more than a few minutes at a time. A flat piece of amethyst can also be used in the same way. But remember, only a few minutes. Do not strain and force this exercise or you might find yourself with a tension headache.

There are many other different types of crystals besides the few I've mentioned. Crystals are without doubt a colorful, positive, enjoyable addition to your life and can only enhance your new self-healing lifestyle. Some people interact very personally with crystals, giving them pet names and recognizing that each has its own distinct personality. There are also many different beliefs on how to charge crystals with energy, such as leaving them for a time in a sunlit windowsill or even using moonlight to charge them. Often, people believe that if you bury crystals in the earth for a time, they will recharge themselves. Some people believe they should be washed in salt water, while others are strongly against crystals getting wet. Try charging and cleaning crystals with any one of these methods for yourself if you feel the need, or create your own method.

You will find lots of good books written about crystals and many wonderful collections worldwide. Your local museum may have its own impressive collection. My professional opinion would be to treat crystals the same way that you treat color. Experiment and explore for yourself. See which ones are good for you and don't just accept what outside sources might say about them.

Like color, crystals also have their own individual vibrations which interact with your own. Crystals may be used to magnify healing positive intent and energies that are used during the healing process. Place the crystal on the area of your body that you are working on. Then place one or both of your hands on top of the crystal. Now just wait and begin to feel the warmth of your own energies and those of the "all that is" which surrounds you becoming magnified and focused. You will learn with time to feel what works for you. Certain crystals will feel good on particular areas of your body.

I cannot end this section about crystals without mentioning the crystal skulls and my own experiences with a couple of them. There are many theories about how the skulls were made and by whom and where they come from. Crystal skulls are said to have been found in Mayan tombs in Mexico and Central America. In the last couple of years, there has been an influx of miniature crystal skulls pouring into the United States from Mexico, Central America and Brazil. These contemporary skulls are made of anything from rose quartz, amethyst, clear quartz, through to jade, and even glass. Max, the Texas crystal skull, was found in Guatemala between 1924 and 1926. Max is the only crystal skull at this time available for public display and touching in the United States. Researchers believe that Max was carved from a 40-50 pound piece of rock clear quartz more than 10,000 years old.

I first heard about Max in 1996. Max is owned privately by Jo Ann Parks in Houston, Texas. Its previous owner was a Tibetan monk and healer. His name was Norbu Chen. Jo Ann worked with Norbu for over seven years. Over time she and her husband became very close to him. Before he died in 1980, he gave them his most treasured possession, a crystal skull. He never told them much about the crystal skull, only that one day when the time was right they would know all about it and what it was for. Jo Ann Parks had witnessed many ceremonies involving Norbu and the skull, and many healing sessions, but after Norbu died, the skull remained in a box in her bedroom closet for seven years.

After watching a television program on crystal skulls, Jo Ann got in touch with Nick Nocerino, who lives in California and is considered the world's foremost authority on crystal skulls. Then she began to learn about the importance of Max. Often people in the presence of skulls have reported healing and uplifting experiences. Others say that their psychic abilities have been enhanced. Jo Ann says that perhaps the most dramatic phenomena which occurs are the holographic images that appear inside of the skulls when they are activated through a combination of light, color, sound or human energy.

I went to visit Max at Jo Ann's home and sat in a room alone with the skull. I realized that Max certainly had a great deal of stored energy and that the skull could be used as a focus point for clairvoyance, rather like a crystal ball. That day, I opened a connection of communication between Max, other crystal skulls and myself. On March 11, 1996 in Austin, Texas, I took part in an event named "A Meeting of Minds." During the session, I first placed my forehead, then both of my hands on Max and the crystal was activated. The whole room seemed to light up and lines of energy were running all across the floor to each corner of the room. I led the group of participants through a healing meditation with the crystal. Afterwards, people came to speak to me about their own healing and uplifting experiences which had occurred for them throughout the event. It was a positive and powerful meeting for me. I worked with the skull to bring many insights for myself and others present.

About a year later, I attended another healing conference, this time with two crystal skulls present. The event was held in Sedona, Arizona, and was called "Healing on the Rocks." It was a two-day weekend seminar. The other crystal skull present is known as Sha-ra-na and was brought by its owner Nick Nocerino, who has the largest known collection of crystal skulls in the world. Again, I took the stage early in the morning with the two skulls present. I laid a hand on each one and performed an activation. The room lit up and was charged. Many people reported healing experiences. For myself, I received all kinds of information and images for both myself personally and for mankind. The skulls' message was both direct and simple: the future is indeed up to us all. More information about the crystal skulls is available on my web site.

My meeting with the crystal skulls was a powerful and enjoyable experience. I later acquired two large pieces of crystal quartz because I realized that basically crystal is enough; skulls are not necessary. I also realized that it is very easy to turn material possessions into icons and I do not feel that this is a necessary or especially positive direction for our awareness to take.

Gemstones

In the early eighteenth century, some colored stones were believed to function medicinally when taken internally, while others worked when applied externally to the body. Many Chinese people even today still use powdered pearls, coral and other gems in their medicine. "Belief in the effects of gemstones on the affairs of man is not new or limited to any specific age or culture, but was part of every human society", says Paul E. Desautels in *The Gem Kingdom*. David Marcum, in *The Dow Jones Erwin Guide to Fine Gems and Jewelry*, reports that over one million people in the United States spend a minimum of $2,000 each on jewelry every year. Marcum also writes about how gemstones are created, saying that metals such as chromium, manganese, vanadium, and iron, which give the dazzling colors of emerald, ruby, and sapphire, were captured during the formation of our solar system; they are bits of galactic debris, the dead remnants of exploded stars and collapsed planetary systems. This may explain why we have a grand fascination with crystals and gemstones and why the vibrations and feelings that they bring to us are enjoyed so much. Perhaps we are reminded of the existences we have experienced in past times.

In ancient times, zodiac signs were associated with a stone that was known to assist and influence individuals. Gemstones were related mystically to the twelve months of the year and the twelve parts of the human body, says Dr.

Morton Walker in *The Power of Color*. Most jewelry stores will be happy to furnish you with a small card showing which gemstone supposedly corresponds to your birth month; for example: January-Garnet, February-Amethyst, and March-Bloodstone or Aquamarine.

I feel that astrology and other sciences have a place in our life especially if we go into them in some detail. But why be an Aquarian or Sagittarian particularly? Why not be all of the signs at the same time or as it suits you? This works well, especially if you look at your horoscope in a morning paper and it does not look too good for the day! So why not choose to be another zodiac sign instead? Now this might sound fun and perhaps even a little irreverent, but my point is why limit yourself with anything? Different astrological signs may tell you for instance the parts of your body that are most likely to be vulnerable and that you need to take care of. For example, people born under the sign of Sagittarius are said to have a vulnerability in their hips and legs; Taureans are opt to put on weight very easily and hold on to tension in their necks and shoulders; Cancerians have a tendency to sink into depression, and the Virgo has a tendency to stomach problems. You do not have to accept these correspondences just because astrology says that they exist, and you don't have to wear a Bloodstone just because you were born in March. Astrology and other sciences are good to explore and to use, but it is also good to ignore or transcend any limitations that they dictate.

I have seen many people who are ill or troubled carrying a special crystal in their pocket or purse and swearing that it has a balancing or healing effect for them and others. Why not, as long as it works for you at the particular time? As with every subject, there will always be data available to prove "for" and "against" the benefits derived or not derived by taking such actions. Crystals exist and are here to be looked at or ignored. The choice is yours. Like everything else in our reality, your own perception at this point is valid, especially if it's really yours, one that you have thought about and felt for yourself.

To conclude, crystals are both fascinating and exciting. They're not necessary to self-healing and can therefore be disregarded. On the other hand, they can also be explored and used. Once again, the choice is yours.

Touch

There is overwhelming evidence that as humans, we need touch in our lives. We thrive with touch, and we become imbalanced without it.

The Touch Research Institute (TRI) is the first center in the world devoted solely to the study of touch and its application in both science and medicine. It was formally established in 1992 by Director Tiffany Field, Ph.D. at the University of Miami School of Medicine. TRI expanded and now has four centers. They are located at the Nova Southeastern University in Florida, in the Philippines, and at the University of Paris.

Touch Points, TRI's quarterly newsletter, reports in its Spring 1998 issue, that at least 30 percent of girls and 10 percent of boys are sexually molested before they are 18 years old. The newsletter also reports that parents and teachers are afraid of touching children because their physical affection might be misinterpreted. Thus children are deprived of touch at a very early age. This is also the reason that many day care centers no longer employ male teachers. The newsletter mentions in its report that the Director of a model preschool in Massachusetts addressed the problem of potential lawsuits against teachers touching preschool children in a national public radio interview. A caller asked her what her teachers would do if a child was hurt on the playground and came running to one of them. She replied rather impassively that her teachers would be advised not to touch or to hold the child.

Several investigators including Dr. Prescott have suggested that touch deprivation in childhood leads to physical violence. He believes that the deprivation of body touch, contact and movement are the basic causes of a number of emotional disturbances including depressive and autistic behaviors, hyperactivities, sexual aberration, drug use, violence and aggression. His theory is that the lack of sensory stimulation in childhood leads to sensory stimulation in adulthood resulting in addiction, delinquency, drug use and crime. Heinicke and Westheimer found that touch deprivation is also harmful to children because it severely affects sleep. In a two-year study, they found touch deprivation caused by periods of separation from parents invariably leads to sleep disturbance in children. Even after children were reunited with their parents after two to twenty weeks, most of the children had difficulty falling asleep or remaining asleep.

The studies about the damaging and harmful effects of touch deprivation are numerous. Enough research has been done over the years to determine that infants, children, adolescents, adults and seniors need touch and that the benefits of touch in our lives are quite substantial. For example, research shows that juveniles suffering from rheumatoid arthritis experienced benefits during and after massage therapy. PMS symptoms are found to be relieved by massage therapy. Adults with multiple sclerosis seem to demonstrate lower anxiety, less depression, better body image, a more positive image of disease progression, and enhanced social function after massage therapy. Young children with atopic dermatitis who were massaged for a month by their parents showed an immediate improvement in their activity level, and parents' anxieties decreased. Significant research has been done with infants with developmental delays, and touch and massage has been noted to have a profoundly positive effect. The infant development team connected to the United Cerebral Palsy in Colorado clearly states that a massage is calming to a cranky and restless child and is an alternative to drugs. It also stimulates active voluntary movement for hypotonic babies, amongst a host of other positive findings.

Many caregivers of the elderly are also now employing touch techniques with their patients and are recommending massage therapy. In February 1995, a study presented at the American Academy of Allergy, Asthma, and Immunology Conference suggests that massage might be part of the answer for asthmatics. Nineteen asthmatics who participated in a three-month pilot test received weekly upper body massage for just fifteen minutes. These participants reported a decrease in chest tightness, wheezing, fatigue and physical pain.

It's clear that a regular massage each week or even every month can be highly beneficial. There are also a growing number of therapists who now use a form of touch known as Touch Therapy. In fact, many nurses have taken the Touch Therapy courses and now use this particular technique.

If you have someone to touch you, don't wait for it to happen. If you feel the need to be touched, ask. If you are alone and do not have others to touch you, bring touch into your life by touching yourself. If there are people close to you who are not used to being touched and hugged, introduce this option gently. Obviously, other peoples' boundaries do need to be recognized and accepted. But it is often surprising how even the most seemingly untouchable people enjoy being touched and hugged if the opportunity is presented at just the right time and in the right way. So be sensitive to others' boundaries, but do not allow boundaries of non-touching to build up between you and others.

Touching can be used in a multitude of ways, and opens both physical and non-physical hearts. Healing does take place. Learning processes are activated by touch. We live in a sensory reality. We are, among other things, sensory beings so it makes sense to accept giving and receiving of touch to others and ourselves. Thankfully, we have come a long way from the ideas fostered in the past by various religions and institutes when touching oneself was considered to be sinful. There were times when individuals never touched or explored their own bodies. Barely an inch of flesh was exposed; to do so would have been deemed improper. Even today, certain religions and cultures believe that lovemaking is solely to be used for the act of procreation, and the man and woman engaging in this activity are each wrapped in a cotton sheet with only the genital areas exposed and free; any touching or sensory enjoyment is frowned upon.

When I see clients for healing sessions, I can see immediately those who are rarely or never touched. Their chest, stomach, throat, forehead, lower back, and upper areas may appear cold, almost like stone. They often have poor circulation with little or almost no energy flowing around the body. Sometimes these people seem closed off, withdrawn and hunched physically into themselves. Others appear as lone, separate units. Initially they seem extremely self-sufficient, but as you look closer you can often see their emotional pain reflected in their eyes. If you look closely at people who are not touched, they appear different, either as very heavy and solid physical figures or as flighty, fly away beings. Either way, such persons are not generally comfortable with relaxing within themselves and opening up.

Gentle exercise is often a good way to get back in touch with your own body and to reconnect with touch, as exercise brings back physical sensation and awareness of the body. I also recommend, if you have privacy, to sit outside in your backyard without clothes on and to feel the sun or gentle wind or even soft rain against your bare body. Allow the body to relax and breathe in this way. If you cannot do this privately outside, you could take time inside the house when you do have privacy and will not be disturbed. If you are living in rather cramped conditions, even to wear no clothes in one room for a few hours, or at least when you go to bed, will allow some sensory awareness to develop. This will lead to further enhanced awareness of touch and sensory perception.

To enhance your extra sensory perception (ESP), which after a while you might agree is not extra at all, but already part of you, try this short exercise with or without your clothes on. Remove your watch, jewelry, shoes, etc. Sit down in a comfortable and relaxed position. Do not cross your arms or legs. Keep your head up. With eyes open or closed, start to breathe through your mouth deeply from your stomach. Take a few minutes to do this. When you are ready, you can begin to visualize opening your ears and noticing all the sounds in and around you. Next, use your sense of smell and concentrate on anything that you smell, distinguishing each and every separate aroma. Now, open your mouth wide and stick out your tongue. Just leave it there for a few moments. No need to feel ridiculous. You are alone. How does it feel? What do you taste in the air? Take your time. When you are ready, put your tongue back in your mouth. Now take a few slow deep breaths and imagine that every single pore of skin on your body is completely wide open. How does that feel? It might feel like a whoosh of energy, a great lightness. You may even become so sensitive that you can almost feel a very small insect or even a particle of dust as it lands on your skin. For a few minutes enjoy the freedom of this exercise. When you have finished, if you wish to close down all the pores of your skin, go ahead by simply visualizing that they do.

There are countless books written about touch and more are appearing frequently. Touch is welcomed as an important part of our world. A small book loved by millions that makes a great gift is *The Little Book of Hugs*. I remember, when living in Cornwall, England, at least twelve years ago, I joined a group of people who were exploring touch and hugging. They practiced the famous sandwich hug, which happens when two adults and one child in the middle have a hug all together. Nowadays, most self-help groups, courses, teachers, participants and therapists are aware of the value of the hug and of touching. By the way, have you ever watched our body language when we hug? It is often very reserved. So come on, if you offer a hug or accept a hug, let yourself go. Enjoy, and really do it like you mean it with your whole being. Develop the enjoyment of closeness and oneness with others. When hearts are open, magic happens.

When we look at touch during the self-healing process and the healing of others, we will find both similarities and differences in the accounts of various healers and individuals. Many healers report that their hands get very hot, warm or even very cold during a session. During my own healing sessions and while watching others, I have paid special attention to the palms of the hands and noticed them lighting up with various colors. Sometimes the palms look like they have lines or vibrations like shots of color or sparks coming from them, almost as if the palms are imprints of colors and vibrations which just need to be activated. A healer friend of mine says that each time he places his hands on a different person, it just takes a moment for them to attune to each other's frequency. Then the vibrations come from the palms of his hand, and the client takes whatever he or she needs. I have also noticed with others and myself, colors coming from the hands and palms flowing through the fingertips. The colors vary with different individuals. It can range from a rainbow mix of colors to purple and gold. Sometimes it almost looks as if silver sparks, like electricity, are coming from the hands and fingers. As you become more sensitive to the touch you give yourself and others, you may also become more aware of colors and vibrations which exist in your palms and fingers.

Touching other life forms besides human beings has value for us all. Have you ever noticed that when you do not feel well, a cat or dog will come and sit on your chest or stomach? These animals are great healers, so enjoy the attention that they give. Often, you will notice that you do feel better as you stroke them, slow down and enjoy their calming vibration. What has happened is that you have not only relaxed and slowed down, but the animal's energy is also being utilized with your own to heal. You are not just petting the animal, but are also giving your own body the time to open up and heal itself. The very action of stroking with your hand massages all of the pressure points on your hand and connects with all other areas in your body. Self-healing is taking place while you are stroking, so during this simple and brief interlude, you are doing yourself good. To love and to caress another being, human or animal, is also to let go and heal ourselves.

Start today to bring touch into your life and watch the boundaries fall away. Touching yourself and others in positive and nurturing ways will be a healthy addition to your life and will accelerate your own self-healing process.

Chapter 6

The Self-Healing Process

&

You may have noticed that I refer throughout this book to illnesses and diseases that are well known. However, it is important to realize that self-healing is not limited to dealing with one particular type of ailment, disease or imbalance at one time, but should also be used to heal both serious and unusual illnesses. You may think that healing a headache is quite different than healing cancer or heart disease. This is true but only in the sense that you will need to be more committed to be well, more committed to refusing to accept the reality in which you find yourself, and to doing whatever it takes to change that situation. You may have bigger fears to deal with than a person with a headache, but you can still face those fears. You will also need to build your self-belief and set aside the conditioning and a lot of what you have been taught which makes you believe that you are not in control and cannot heal. Start today and give yourself a chance; you probably realize already that you have nothing to lose and everything to gain. Miracles, as we call them, will and do happen.

Expecting the best

One of the first steps in the self-healing process is to

expect the best. If you are generally in good health, a good time to start with self-healing is now, by simply expecting to stay in good health. For example, just because you have a history of heart disease or cancer in your family, this does not automatically mean that this will happen to you despite statistics telling you otherwise. Have you noticed in the last few years how many more people are becoming focused on diseases and illness that have been present in past family members? There is almost an expectation of experiencing the same health problems. Today, it seems to be one of the first criteria to be considered even before illness happens, whereas a few years ago, the expectation of contracting hereditary disease was considered only after everything else was taken into account.

This does not mean that noting the existence of the hereditary factor is a bad idea, only that it can become a solid mental block for many people. Decide now to break the pattern. This is an important point. I have met numerous people who have lived for years with the fear and expectation of these diseases happening to them. This fear acts like a magnet, drawing the negative situation to oneself and creating the very reality that is feared. You are creating your own reality, so decide today that heart disease, cancer and other so-called hereditary diseases are not going to happen to you despite however many occurrences you have in your family history. Make the choice. Remember that your thoughts are even more powerful factors in what does actually take place, than statistics could possibly ever be. You can make the decision within yourself of what will be and what will not be in your own future.

Be aware that expectation of illness is an acceptance and conditioning within ourselves, such as expecting a cold because those around you have one, expecting to have an allergy because you are constantly bombarded with the message on television that it's "high pollen season," or expecting to catch a virus or germs when visiting someone in a hospital. It only takes a moment to decide that this is not how your reality will be. Expect the best, and you will receive the best.

Empathizing—Knowing yourself

While you are healing yourself or helping others to heal, it is essential to become more aware of your own thoughts and feelings on a daily basis, and to be aware of thoughts and emotions that you have picked up from others. This will help you to stop empathizing with others, feeling their pains and emotions as your own, and allow yourself to feel and be more in control, centered and energized.

To start becoming aware of your own thoughts and feelings, and to separate them from others, try this exercise first thing in the morning as you wake up. Ask yourself: "How am I today? How do I feel?" You might feel that you are fine or great, or perhaps you just feel blank, with nothing in particular on your mind or in your emotions. If you feel blank, it is quite likely that you are totally present in the moment.

What tends to happen next is that you question the validity of this blankness and then you bring everything that happened the day before or earlier into this blank moment. At this point, you feel how you "were," rather than exactly how you "are" in the here and now, and you become bogged down in many ways. Depending on your current lifestyle, this might feel like walking on a never-ending treadmill, a "here I go again" feeling, even an oppressive feeling, or it might be an excitement about having so much to do and accomplish.

You do not have to be a prisoner of your initial feelings. If you do feel bad, ask yourself why and make the decision to deal with it as soon as possible. Ask yourself what you need to do and then take action as soon as you can. Value your wellness and commit yourself to bringing changes when necessary.

On the other hand, if you wake up feeling great, enjoy the

feeling and stay with it. Don't be afraid to feel great in case it does not last; just accept and enjoy it now. The point of this exercise is to become aware of how you are at the beginning of each day. Later on, perhaps at mid-morning, ask yourself again: "How am I? How do I feel right now?" You can then see how different you feel since you first woke. Then you can look back at your day and pinpoint who you met, what you did, and all the events that brought you to your present feelings. By doing this you can begin to pinpoint how other people and situations affect your mood, and what is really yours, and what is not. Practice this exercise for two to three weeks. After that, just do it occasionally, to stay on track with your own awareness of how you are really feeling and why.

When you find yourself around aggressive, angry people or someone who drains you, or in places that have a negative down effect on you, use this visualization: Imagine yourself quickly being surrounded by light and color. I say quickly because this does not have to take long. You do not have to feel, see or imagine the light or color in a vivid solid way, if this does not come easily to you at first. The outline thought is powerful enough. This light and color that you imagine might be in the shape or form of a pyramid, a bubble, a circle, a cloud, or anything else where you can feel protected and enveloped. This visualization works really well if you are in a draining work situation or have to work in a place with no windows or natural air and light. The visualization is also beneficial when you are out of balance or going through a healing process. While you are imagining yourself being surrounded by a beautiful bright light in the shape of a pyramid, a bubble, a cloud or any other shape of your choice, make sure that your creation starts above the top of your head and ends well below your feet.

By doing this exercise, you will still draw to yourself vibrations and energies that are around you, and you will still send out to the world and other people everything you wish and need. But you will have formed a filtering system and will be drawing to yourself vibrations of a more positive and higher nature, simply because you have taken action, have become more focused, and have greater expectations.

Dealing with your emotions

A part of your self-healing new lifestyle is giving to yourself and accepting gifts. We are not machines. More and more people are realizing that they cannot continue concentrating on others and not themselves. Most of this section is about what we all know, but need to be reminded of from time to time as we get overloaded and overwhelmed with our work, our families and hundreds of different stresses within the various phases of our lives. Taking time out seems to be the most important aspect of self-healing for most people. This can seem impossible when you have a tight schedule, but remember, time is yours, and if you don't seem to have enough already, you will have to take time for yourself. Unfulfilled needs cause chaos in our lives so it is worthwhile to take the time to recognize that we have needs and to fulfill them.

Start today. Relax, be still, and ask yourself: "what do I really need?" Your needs might be simple. If they are big, begin a plan for how to fulfill them, even if it will take some time. Meanwhile, make a start and fulfill those needs on a smaller scale. Recently I asked a group of people how they treat themselves. The responses I received came from both men and women. Here are some of the answers I received:

- I treat myself from time to time with a massage, a trip to the theater and a meal out.
- I take the phone off the hook and sometimes treat myself to a facial.
- I walk for a couple of miles by myself or read.
- Being kind to someone else makes me feel good and

gives me fuel to fulfill my own dreams.
- I have a Yoga retreat once a year or a massage.
- I think positive thoughts and drink iced cappuccino.
- I get a haircut; I tidy up or buy a present for a friend or myself.
- I go horseback riding, sit in a hot bath and drink a glass of wine.
- I go and watch my favorite football team play and better still, we win!
- I buy a beautiful diamond.
- I get away from all human contact and get in touch with nature.
- I go to the movies and eat dark chocolate.
- I soak my feet in hot water with a few drops of essential oils.

You can make your own list. This action alone will give you some perspective on how well you fulfill your own needs.

Sometimes a gift to yourself might not be material. It could be a change in thinking, like "stop being so perfect with yourself in all that you do," or the opposite, "stop accepting the mediocre and second best, be more demanding." Giving and accepting gifts for yourself could be giving yourself the gift of love. One woman wrote that she had just met someone new and for the first time in many years she was giving herself permission to love and be loved. Caring about yourself, believing in yourself, and allowing yourself to be both right and wrong is another gift to yourself.

If you have reached the point where one day runs into another and you hardly remember what you enjoy anymore, it is time to stop and listen to yourself. Other signs might include often feeling stressed, suffering from headaches, aches and pains, allergies and illness which cannot be identified by either yourself or medical professionals, losing patience even with those you care about, sleeping too much, finding it difficult to be still, to concentrate and to sleep. It might help to remember everything that you enjoy, all that gives you pleasure both big and small, and make a list. Keep the list near by, cross the items off as you make time and enjoy them again. This list will serve as a reminder to take the time for yourself until it becomes a part of your life and a priority even when your life is at its busiest.

Putting yourself first initially might be a treat in itself, but as time goes by and you find that you are happier, healthier, and more balanced, you will realize that it is not a luxury but a vital part of you which needs to be expressed. On a spiritual level, deep needs also take time to be discovered and fulfilled. Connecting on a heart level with a friend or even a stranger can give a great sense of freedom, openness and wholeness, bringing you back to yourself, a powerful place to be. For some, fulfilling needs on a spiritual level might be a meaningful meditation, perhaps listening to a beautiful or exciting piece of music, or being outside and at one with nature. The different ways of fulfilling spiritual and emotional needs are endless. We will each have our own preferences. The emotional part of us needs to love and be loved. Find a way to express this part of you. If you are in a relationship where this need is not being fulfilled, start to bring change today by asking yourself why you have chosen this path. Be honest with yourself. If you feel alone, make friends with the alone part of you. Do not be afraid of it or avoid it any longer. The hard fact is that, as long as you hate or fear your loneliness, you are prolonging it. Loneliness will leave when you no longer need to experience it.

Each one of us has strong and powerful emotions. The more we resist them, the more often they come up and the more miserable we feel with ourselves when we run away from them and feel overpowered by them. I recommend the following exercise when you are feeling an intense emotion and you want to reach the end of it. Take a deep breath and lie down on the couch, bed or floor or even on the ground outside. Allow yourself to feel the intense emotion you are experiencing, whether it is anger, loneliness, despair, fear or sadness. I mention the emotions which people generally do not like to feel; however, you can use this exercise to go through pleasurable emotions too. Now breathe deeply from the very bottom of your stomach and allow this emotion to wash all over you and all through your body. Keep breathing deeply through your mouth. If you feel the emotion in your stomach or chest, place a hand on these areas to rub, soothe, relax, and do whatever feels good. If you need to curl into a ball and rock yourself, do so. Go with your feelings and do whatever it takes, but don't give up. The feeling does have an end, so keep going. When you feel enveloped and overwhelmed, but in charge because of the breathing and your commitment of getting to the end of the emotion, then you can say "enough." If you are dealing with unpleasant emotions, now is the moment to tell yourself "no more pain." Just say it clearly in your mind twice. When you are at the end of a particular feeling and emotion, ask yourself, What is beyond this now? Keep your eyes closed. How does the emotion and feeling look? What picture, color, thought or idea comes into your mind? Remember, even the smallest thing can be important, so make a mental note. When you have a picture or feeling, ask yourself what it means. What is it telling you? Practice is the key, and commitment to yourself is important. At first, sitting down and taking these few steps might seem like hard work. But realize that you are worth the time and effort.

Knowing yourself and how you act and react is an important aspect of self-healing and wholeness. It means that by taking time you are going forward to a far greater reward—happiness, wholeness, peace and realization of yourself and all that you are. Taking time and giving gifts to yourself is a recipe for good health, balance and wholeness, and a necessary part of the self-healing process.

Chakra system and beyond

Chakra is a Sanskrit word that means "wheel of spinning energy." The teaching of the Chakra system seems to go back over 4,000 years. Although it is commonly accepted today that the human body has seven major chakras, references to many more can be found in ancient texts. The fact that the original complex energy system has been reduced to seven chakra points, also known as energy centers, is an indication that these particular points are to be used only as a reference and focus rather than as an absolute.

Chakras, or energy centers—however you prefer to call them—are a fast way for you to focus on various parts of your body and receive an overall view of how you are, physically and emotionally. Using specific points also gives you a reference to see and decide which areas of your body might need some work, using your own self-healing techniques. I will also present my own revised Chakra system which works equally as well to show that you do not have to stick to a specific formula. I hope it will also inspire and encourage you to create your own version of reference points throughout the body. But first let's look briefly at the energy centers that are generally mentioned and their accepted functions:

The base or root chakra is located at the base of the spine; it is considered to be a place of power where life force is stored.

The spleen or sacral chakra is located in the lower abdomen area; it is generally associated with sexual energy.

The solar plexus chakra is located in the stomach area; it is used to connect with others and to tune into your own immediate needs and emotions.

The chest chakra, known as the heart center, also stores emotional feelings and is used as a way to open, relate and connect with others.

The throat chakra is the center of communication.

The brow chakra, at the center of the forehead, is also known as the "Third Eye"; it is usually associated with psychic intuition and often viewed as a tool to gather impressions and information.

The crown chakra is located at the top of your head; it is your connection to the universe and "all that is."

Many books and teachers say that each chakra is a particular color. From experience, I have seen that this is not the case. I also do not agree with the idea that clairvoyance and psychic abilities are only or predominantly connected and perceived by the "Third Eye" or forehead center.

Go with what you feel, perceive and form your own opinion. You will find that different clairvoyants may perceive your chakras in different ways, colors and shapes. This really is fine as it is just a matter of perception, and perception is not fixed. Later, in chapter 9, we will look at the use of color when applied to the chakras during a self-healing session.

You can incorporate the Chakra system into your everyday life. It is a system that works very simply. It is also very old and can be complex. Many books are available to help you if you wish to investigate the subject further. I personally use the Chakra system in a simple way. All systems can be simple or complex; I prefer simplicity.

My revised version of the basic Chakra system includes the stomach, chest, throat, forehead and crown chakras, and four other chakra points not generally used: the back of the head, the shoulders, the ears and the kidney area. I include the back of the head as a place where realization occurs to us when we process knowledge. It is a point where tension is often stored and headaches are created. The shoulders are a point where much tension is also stored, generally from the recent past, times and events. You or a professional massage therapist can massage both of these areas and release the accumulated pressure. I introduce the ears as a chakra point as they are used for balance. When one of the ears is out of balance, it is often due to a block in one or both of the ears. The block may be so subtle as to be barely noticeable, but it can have an effect on the corresponding side of the body, i.e. left ear, left side. If you are particularly sensitive, you can feel your ears rebalancing and clearing themselves. This often happens automatically after imbalance has occurred. The kidneys are another important area of your body to massage and on which to concentrate your self-healing focus. They are a part of the body's own natural clearing system and can become blocked by both physical and emotional toxins.

With a little practice, you will find that even when you are not especially relaxed, you can go through these centers very fast with your mind and feel or see if they are clear or blocked. I will show you in chapter 9 how to clear them very quickly when necessary with just a thought. Clearing your chakras requires a little time and practice, but will become a useful tool, one that is at your disposal instantly.

Implosion and Explosion

I believe that our bodies are in a constant state of implosion (a bursting inwards) and explosion (a bursting outwards) which we can link to the constant action of breathing in and breathing out, although breathing is not the only catalyst of implosion and explosion. We might call the rate of imploding and exploding a "vibratory pattern." This is why I mentioned earlier the importance of having a real sense of our own individual time, as I believe we all vibrate, e.g. implode and explode, in our own unique time space. Presently, science tells us that it is still difficult to define and to measure scientifically what physical matter really is. It would seem then that we are still not totally sure of what is solid and what is not. I feel that when we implode, we take in non-formed and formed matter, and when we explode we let go of physical and non-physical matter and become once again without form. When you focus on a fixed point in a mirror, for example, as suggested in the mirror exercise in chapter 9, you will at some point have the experience of seeing and not seeing yourself in the mirror. You will literally appear and disappear. You are watching the natural manifestation of imploding and exploding taking place.

The overload of the physical body, emotions and the nervous system can slow down this natural imploding-exploding process quite quickly. We begin to have a build-up of physical and non-physical matter that contains thoughts, feelings and emotions, as well as past, present and future events; in other words, all of the created and uncreated realities of ourselves and others. This build-up also contains an overload of the "all that is" in its formless state. When this overload occurs, we have a body and form that is no longer imploding and exploding at its own natural speed. This is where letting go, self-expression and creativity need to be used; otherwise we have what we call an imbalance, which may express itself in physical, mental and emotional problems.

An efficient way to let go of the overload is a rebirthing. When one undergoes a rebirthing session, the breathing connects the individual more deeply and intensely with the imploding and exploding process. At the end of the session, the individual often feels hundreds or even thousands of small pinpricks of light or energy, often experienced as "tingling" throughout the body. It seems that having reached a heightened sense of awareness, these people's implosive and explosive process has been further activated and they have become more in tune with the physical sensations caused by the activation. We'll look at the rebirthing in more detail in the next chapter.

We can stimulate, intensify and activate the natural implosion and explosion constantly taking place in our body; the constant bringing in to us what we need and the letting go of what we don't need. A simple way is to use the chakra points or energy centers previously mentioned, such as the stomach, the chest, the throat, the forehead, the crown, the ears, the kidneys or whichever other area of your body you feel drawn to start with. Remember that the chakra points, energy centers, or focus points do not necessarily need to be any more important than any other area of the body, unless we accept using them as reference points for clearing and balancing work to take place.

To work with reference points, place your flat hand on your chosen body area and begin to massage with slow circular movements, first moving for a while in one direction, then in the other direction. Next, you may feel the desire to gently move your hand again backwards and forwards, up and down the area you chose. This gentle massage will stimulate and activate the many energy points of your body. Implosion and explosion becomes intensified, and physical and emotional toxins are released.

A clear illustration of this mechanism is rubbing your stomach when you have a stomachache. Do you remember as a small child, when you had "tummy ache," the teacher or your mother told you to rub it and make it better? And you placed your small hand on your stomach and rubbed around and around, and then up and down, and indeed your "tummy ache" did get better. When we are out of balance, or have an illness, a clear focus of energy needs to be re-established both inside and outside of our bodies. The exercise "Opening your senses" in chapter 9, in which you are instructed to open every pore of your body, also illustrates how the activation of implosive and explosive process feels.

I believe that memories also intensify our own implosive and in turn explosive process. Think of those days when you find yourself remembering one past event after another, almost like reliving a series of film clips. It could be that on those days we are using the strings of memories to fuel and intensify our implosive and explosive process, which in turn is a major part of the clearing and healing process. Interestingly, psychiatry and psychology use a form of therapy called "implosive therapy" in which the patient is given massive exposure to extreme anxiety-arousing stimuli in order to extinguish anxiety associated with the entire class of the stimuli. The patient can also be directly exposed to cues reminiscent of past trauma. By subjecting himself to a flood of stimuli, and by bringing forth past memory, the patient is in fact creating a situation where implosion and explosion is intensified, which theoretically should lead to balance and the letting go of overload.

Another manifestation of an imbalance in the implosion and explosion process can be seen in the stomach. This is one of the first areas where we generally accept weight gain. This weight gain is used almost as a protective element and shield to cover, nurture and even hold in a build-up of thoughts, emotions and negative feelings within this emotional center. When normal implosion does not occur because we are holding on to matter which is acting as a shield and stopping the "letting go" from happening, we have a backlog. Then in some way an exploding process needs to happen to clear this backlog, often as a real outburst of emotion or expression, which can take some time to happen, as the protruding stomach becomes more and more of a protective force. Many people will be able to relate to the protruding stomach issue. Even people who are usually thin also have times when they are stressed and worried and are holding on to emotions, and they too develop protruding stomachs.

There are ways to bring back the balance of implosion and explosion within our bodies and our minds. One of the easiest ways to clear the stomach, the emotional center, is to lie on the floor, relax, allow yourself to feel that you are flowing and to have this thought in mind: "I am letting go of everything I no longer need." I highly recommend doing this at the end of the day or before going to sleep. You will really notice a difference the next day. At night your body will continue the letting go process, as you have already pro-grammed it with your thoughts to do so. This exercise can be used by everyone, whether thin, overweight or in between.

I also see the protruding stomach, to a degree, as a matter of people exploding outwardly and visibly rather than the process taking place normally both inside and outside of the physical body. This happens simply because clearing and releasing has not happened often and quickly enough. Hence the build-up.

The stomach area is known as the seat of emotions. On a physical level, I see the stomach as a holding area for implosive material, that material we know as food. As we are all different, we each have different foods or other sub-stances which at times makes us literally stomach sick. I believe that when you want to be stomach sick, you actually want to remove alien and foreign particles and matter from the stomach. As we are all unique and have our own individ-ual blueprints and body chemistry, what makes us sick and needs to be removed will be different for each one of us. But our bodies do know and are aware of the balance needed; therefore, it makes sense to eat what your body feels is right rather than what you have been told is good for you. Different foods act as protection for the stomach for differ-ent people. The humble apple is a perfect example. There is a formula within the make-up of an apple which lines and protects the stomach from the negative effects and build-up that other foods and substances leave in the stomach. Hence the saying, "An apple a day keeps the doctor away."

There is no doubt that there are many other foods which work in this way. However, I feel it is important for individuals to experiment and find what works for them, as an excess of something that we are told works is not necessarily the best idea either. For example, the concentration in juice such as orange juice and the habit of drinking this each day may not be the best balance for some individuals, although it may work for others. So doing what we have been told is good for us and what is actually good for us can be very different for each individual.

Breathing

Deep breathing, taking long slow deep breaths from the bottom of the stomach, is a process I mention often throughout this book. To breathe is to live. On a metaphysical level, I use the idea that each time you breathe in, you breathe in the "all that is." And each time you breathe out, you breathe out all that you no longer need. It works. I also mention breathing as an activator of the implosion and explosion healing process, whereby unneeded foreign matter is expelled from the body. On a basic physiological level, we are told that a deep abdominal breath increases the oxygen supply to the brain and musculature and stimulates the branch of the autonomic nervous system that promotes a state of calmness and quiescence. Deep breathing also helps to excrete toxic substances through the lungs.

Breathing is used in many disciplines, such as yoga, meditation and mind control exercises. Different systems have been used in various cultures throughout time. Recently in Russia, for example, two scientists, Professor Vladimir Frolov and Professor Eugine Kustov disclosed a technique and process called endogenic breathing. The theory of endogenic breathing is based on the recent medical research of another Russian, Professor Georgi Petrakovich's hypothesis of breathing. It has been promoted as a way to develop longevity, the increased life span of human beings.

There are also some people who believe that the breath

is a life force and that by breathing deeply each day in a specific way we can revitalize and rejuvenate the body and feed ourselves, even to the point of eliminating the need for food. These people are known as breatharians. It would seem there is still much more for us to discover about the breath and breathing.

At this time, I would suggest researching the positive benefits of breathing for yourself by simply using deep breathing in the exercises included in this book. I also recommend taking at least ten minutes every day to breathe deeply from the stomach, preferably outside in the open air. Include deep breathing in your life and observe the positive benefits for yourself; view it as another useful tool in your collection of self-healing techniques.

Meditation

Webster's dictionary defines meditation as: "continued or extended thought; reflection; contemplation." It also mentions "transcendental meditation; devout religious contemplation or spiritual introspection." For some people, meditation has a specific meaning; for others it may bring to mind a collection of thoughts and images such as the cross-legged guru, possibly dressed in white, sitting straight, eyes focused into the distance as if in deep space, or perhaps a guru and master with closed eyes and a peaceful expression. If you are not familiar with meditation, you might even feel intimidated by the term.

There are many different regimes, disciplines and forms of meditation. Meditation has many associations with other cultures and religions, especially in the Far East and Middle East, and has been used from ancient times to find inner calm and peace, to transcend the everyday, to find oneself and to expand beyond the self. There are countless books and other aids to understanding and practicing meditation. In this section, I will keep the subject basic and simple. The important point to remember is that meditation is an experience and a tool that is already part of you. It is nothing to be afraid of; it is not complicated or beyond understanding.

To use meditation within your own self-healing process, I suggest you consider first the places where you have experienced moments when you are still, like sitting in the yard in the sun or cool evening air, or taking a walk in the early morning or evening. Or it might be the stillness you feel while fishing, or doing paperwork late at night when everyone else is in bed. There are indeed many moments when we enjoy meditation in our own ways, without necessarily thinking about it. Meditating is essentially being still. This does not mean that a cross-legged posture or any other particular posture must be observed. If you decide that you want quietness and stillness to connect with yourself, to quiet your mind and be aware of where and how you are right now, I would recommend the following meditation:

Choose your own quiet space. Remove watches, jewelry and shoes, and loosen any restrictive clothing. Sit comfortably. Keep your head up. Allow your hands to be comfortable resting on your knees. With your eyes open or closed, begin to relax by taking long slow deep breathes from the bottom of your stomach. Do not try to clear your mind, or think about anything in particular. Only focus on your breathing for now. Just allow thoughts to come and go. Stay in this position for ten minutes or so, allowing yourself to be still. At the end of this meditation, if you wish to think positive affirmations or thoughts, do so. Use color to surround and bathe yourself in and then breath the color and thought into and through your body.

You can use this simple exercise for just ten minutes each

day or every other day and add nothing more. You could also add to your session once or twice a week by using the exercise in chapter 9 for clearing your chakras or energy centers.

Clearing your mind is also very beneficial as it allows you to let go of the old, leaving room for the new. If you decide that you want to use meditation to clear your mind, get ready as in the previous exercise, sit comfortably, relax and take long slow deep breathes from the bottom of your stomach. But this time focus your gaze on a faceted crystal, a burning candle, the red glowing lighted end of an incense stick, a mark on the wall, or any fixed point which catches your attention. Keep looking at this point and allow your thoughts to come and go while gazing at this point and breathing slowly and deeply. When you are ready, have the thought clearly and strongly twice in your mind: "I am letting go of everything I no longer need." If your eyes feel heavy or you want to close them at any point, go ahead and do so. Continue breathing and feeling relaxed. Notice what is in your mind. If there is a color there that you like, expand it and enjoy it. If there is a symbol or a picture, accept it and ask yourself what it means. If there is nothing, a blank or a black space, imagine you are diving into the nothingness and blank space and enjoy the freedom of that. If you feel like flying, see yourself as a bird or as you are now and let yourself fly. Do whatever you feel, until you feel that you have finished.

You can keep your meditation very simple and be only still. Or you can add countless other exercises to it. Follow suggested exercises and traditional ones found in books, or use your own thoughts, ideas and creativity. You can enjoy and find value in meditation during your everyday life. At the very least, find a time to be with yourself, to be calm and still, to release, to strengthen and to heal.

The self-healing process works. We have looked

throughout this chapter at several major elements which may be useful or even necessary in your own healing process. However, you do not need to turn your self-healing process into a regime that must be rigorously adhered to. Rather, use the tools and elements as and when needed, making time to include the various aspects and considerations into your lifestyle. The more committed you are to yourself and the more chance you give yourself to heal, the more positive results you will have. Decide to be open to wellness and wholeness. Believe that it is your right, your choice and your reality and it will become so. Always be kind with yourself and patient with your own development of awareness. Truly realize that you will arrive where you need to be at exactly the right moment.

Chapter 7

Letting Go

⌘

An important part of becoming healthy and staying in balance is letting go of tension, stress and deeply buried or surface negative emotions such as anger, frustration, fear, hurt, pain and hate. I mentioned these so-called negative emotions because I have not yet found anyone who was ill or out of balance because he or she was living in or holding onto an abundance of joy and love. However, people are often ill because of the loss of joy and love from their lives; some have never known either of these emotions.

Although I always look at each person as a unique individual being, and never apply generalities to anyone, it is possible to recognize patterns and links between some illnesses and certain emotions or mix of emotions. For example, lower backache, cancer, rheumatism, and irritable bowel syndrome are often linked with holding on to anger, pain and fear. I'm not suggesting that these illnesses are not very real in the body, but that letting go of these emotions is necessary to initiate and to allow the healing process to move towards completion. I include in chapter 10 the case of an elderly European couple who came to the United States for a retreat. The woman had had rheumatism in her hand and wrist for many years, but she healed during her stay and has not had the problem since. This is an example of a person who finally learns to let go of pain she has been holding on to. She let go by expressing herself, opening herself to be healed and making a strong commitment to herself that she would no longer accept pain in her life. Later she became aware of how much she had been always surrounded by others' pain and that a big cause of the rheumatism had been her empathizing with others, feeling powerless to help them and taking their pain into herself instead. It was almost like a self-punishment for not having the answers to help the ones she cared about.

If you are in perfect health and shape you have found ways to let go already or not to hold on to what you do not need. You let go quite naturally. When you were young and carefree perhaps you let go of things more easily and never seemed to be ill; you were excited then and busy exploring life. There is some truth in the idea of not having time to be ill, a philosophy that works for many people. But as time goes by, letting go is often not so easy or spontaneous. Perhaps we simply do not make time for it; we get over-loaded. Some people become more relaxed once again in their older years. They live life from a more relaxed per-spective believing that the smaller events and problems that they used to worry about are no longer really important: "Time is running out, might as well make the most of it!" Such sentiments are played then in their minds.

In this chapter we will look at some ways for you, the individual, to let go. You will also find exercises in chapter 9 that will help you get in touch with your own letting go process.

Self-Sabotage

We are often afraid that we cannot have or keep some-thing that we want very much. So rather than go through expected loss or disappointment, we sabotage the possible positive reality without even giving it an option to be realized and enjoyed. We are more open and used to losing something good than we are to keeping it. This way of doing is a learned pattern and a defensive mechanism that we can switch around. We can change our reality, and become used to triumph rather than disappointment. Start today. As you become less defensive, life becomes more wonderful.

Before you discard negative emotions from your life, give yourself the chance to feel each one of them. Then you will find yourself no longer fearing or running away from negative emotions, rather choosing not to experience negative emotion very often, if at all. Life can be happier and more joyful more of the time if you choose from experience and knowledge rather than from fear or from the feeling that you cannot or do not want to handle negative reality.

If you continue to sabotage yourself, you need to look deeper into your own self-image and perceive how you actually value and see yourself. Perhaps you will need to dig deeper and deal with unresolved core issues that take you away from valuing and loving yourself. These issues can prevent you from having what you want and need, keeping you from truly realizing that you really can be blissful and happy.

Tragedies and dramas

We hear inspiring stories of people who have been close to death and came back quite changed. Birth and death are such profound experiences that, as we witness them or are a part of them, we often react by letting go of much within ourselves that we do not need. Natural disasters, wars and other dangerous situations, and great or small personal tragedies and challenges can also have the same affect. Think about tragedies again, both big and small, that have happened to you and to others. At first when they are happening to you, it may not be easy to see the reasons or the positive side of them. But as time goes by, if you open your-self to look again, you will see how and why they happened. There are always positives as well as negatives. I am not saying that you should immediately feel happy when you feel that your life is falling apart and that you are losing everything; I am saying that there are also much greater joys for you to find on your path. When one door closes, another opens. But we must first move away from the idea of punishment and reward. This is a self-limiting concept and not necessarily how reality is.

If you are in a tragedy, catastrophe or devastating time in your life right now, when you decide that you can, try this short exercise: Sit down and be still, breathe deeply from your stomach, breathing through your mouth. No matter what is going through your mind, mentally create and see an image of yourself being completely involved in your current situation, then see yourself taking two definite large steps backwards. Now stop and look again at the scene that you have been totally absorbed in. Look at it in detail, if you wish, for a few moments. But do not allow yourself to be pushed back into it, rather keep those two steps away. Observe, and see if you notice anything else that was not there before. If you see yourself being broken and beaten down, mentally pull this "you" up straight, love and nurture this "you" and give this "you" strength. I am not suggesting that this will immediately change everything, but it will help. At the very least it will bring some perspective and give you a feeling of control over what may have seemed moments ago a totally out of control situation.

Letting go every day
Letting go needs to be a part of your everyday life. For maximum benefit, I would recommend that you include let-ting go even in small ways every few days from now on. If you want to do something every day, a strong thought in

your mind twice a day, such as "I am letting go of everything I no longer need," will be of enormous benefit. You will also then get into the mental and physical habit of letting go more readily and easily. Because you will not have such a build-up in your body and mind to deal with all at once, you will find it easier to reach and recall past events and reactions that you need to let go of as well. You will also then be clear more of the time and take in more of what you need and draw to yourself.

Positive affirmations work. We are very much what we think. Thoughts are vibrations and we are vibrations. Practice positive thinking and make it a part of your life. Sometimes people practice positive thought and affirmation without seeing much change. The key is to focus your positive thought in the present moment. For example, to say: "I am a free and powerful being" is quite different than saying: "each day I become a free and powerful being." Words are as important and as powerful as thoughts, so be aware of what you think and what you say. Time and time again, we hear people who want something very badly but think it probably won't happen. Even when they get what they really want they might say: "it will probably all fall apart because of my luck," or "it might not last." Luck does not have anything to do with positive thoughts or affirmations. Luck is a word used to describe a reality of connected events that have not yet been examined. It's an explanation for not having thought and looked at how life actually works.

Taking control is a good positive step for letting go. When we do this, we feel good. Start with your surroundings. Take a good look at where you live and go through your possessions. Now throw away, sell, or give away everything you no longer need and everything that is broken or that you kept for a later day. You can always acquire material possessions again if you really need them. Just by taking this small step you will be making space, not just in your home, but within yourself, because the place where you live or stay at this moment is a reflection of you. So make it the best and the most workable for you whether you intend to be in that space for a day or a lifetime. Make this action a part of your life especially when you feel stuck or when nothing much appears to be moving in your life. You will be delighted with the positive changes that you bring.

There are many ways to use everyday situations to clear your mind and being. For instance, motion is an easy and simple way to let go. If you are by a running stream or any kind of moving water, take a minute to gaze into the water and let yourself relax. Now imagine you are letting any stress and tension go with the water as it flows forward. Have the usual thought in mind once or twice: "I am letting go of everything I no longer need." This is all you need to do. You can do the same by simply repeating the process after turning on the cold-water tap. Just let yourself go for a few minutes until you feel that it is enough. From time to time I like to stand at a bus stop and use the same technique for a few minutes as I watch the traffic go by. If you try this, allow your gaze to follow the traffic, having the thought in mind: "I am letting go of everything I no longer need." Just allow yourself to feel "you" flowing forward. If you are sitting at an outside pavement café, you can use the same technique simply by watching people go by. These techniques only take a few minutes of your time, until you feel relaxed and calm. Initially, do not expect to feel clear and empty right away, and do not look for visible outside signs that the process is complete. Trust that the process works without these outside pointers. There is no proper or correct amount of time to let go. Only go with what you feel. Trust that there are parts of you at work that you may not feel in a physical way. After a while, you will notice that you feel relaxed, alert and generally more in tune and open to new thoughts and ideas.

A brilliant and simple way to let go in your own time and space is to write. Start today by taking a blank piece of paper and write. What you write does not have to make sense or mean anything in particular. Start with what you are wearing, how you feel, or random thoughts. Let them come. If you cannot think of anything at all and nothing just comes, fill the blank space by writing your own name over and over again.

You can keep your writings or throw them away. The point is not what you create, but the action in itself. It's a way to let go and move again in the flow of life and your own being. After a week or two you might be surprised to see that you do have things to say in your writing which make a lot of sense. But initially the exercise is rather like taking a lid off a boiling pot; it allows the steam to be released. You may not even realize that you are like a boiling pot and in need of release, because the boiling may have been going on deep inside of you for a long time. So writing is a good way to take the lid off your emotions, and allow realizations that are inside of you to come to the surface.

In various forms of bodywork touch is used for release. Try a professional massage at least once. You may enjoy the session and benefit so much that you make it a part of your life. Massage therapists work with all different types of bodies, so feel free to reveal yours. Memories are stored in our cells and body tissues; muscles also hold pain and tension. As you relax more during a massage session, you might have the experience of day-dreaming, drifting from one reality to another. Some people become aware of flashes from past times, even other lives or future times. Allow these thoughts to come and go unless you feel that a particular picture, color or feeling that you received as a certain part of you was touched, is really important. In this case, remember it, and when you have a quiet time and can give the matter full attention, ask yourself questions about what you felt or saw. Always remember that you do have the answers, so just keep going until they come, whether immediately or in a few days. Sometimes answers travel from deep forgotten parts of ourselves and need time to surface.

Sexual Tension

Sexual tension and release is a normal and natural part of our lives. You may find sexual healing a powerful, even perhaps illuminating tool for your own self-healing process. Please note that I am not saying that everyone should express himself or herself sexually. The choice is yours, but realize that there is always a choice.

If you are alone or do have a sexual partner, remember there are times when self-release is both comforting and freeing. Take a long scented bath; use soft lighting or candles and perhaps relaxing music. After a luxurious soak, move on to a warm or cool comfortable space. Use some oil or lotion and explore your body; be accepting and loving of it with no judgments. Touch yourself in ways that feel good. Let yourself go and give yourself permission to feel good and release built-up sexual tension and stress. You do not have to be a non-sexual being because you do not have a sexual partner.

If there are parts of your body that you do not like, welcome them by stroking, nurturing, loving, and touching these parts. Try taking off all of your clothes and standing in front of a full-length mirror. Now just look at all of your body. If you find yourself disliking certain parts, stop the thought immediately, touch, and send that part love and acceptance instead. A faster way to bring change is to accept and love yourself, not only for what you are becoming or wish to be, but as you are now.

Stress

Stress seems today to play a large part in our life. We might believe we are stressed because we do too much and have too much going on in our lives. But if we look again, we will see that this may not be the case. It could be that we have a far greater capacity for doing and being without experiencing stress than we realize. Stress may be the effect of functioning without enough self-expression, to the point of holding ourselves back and holding ourselves in. When this is the case, we may feel as if we are functioning on automatic, rather than participating actively in life.

Think of it this way: each day we gather more and more of the "all that is" material. We gather it automatically. The sole purpose of this gathering process is to express and create that which we take in. When we do not express and create we have a build-up. Anger and frustration are signs that stress needs to be released. The same is true of weight gain, and possibly a protruding stomach. If you locate the particular stress points in your body, you can gently massage, touch, or exert pressure to them and release stress. Crying and body movement are both good release processes for removing stress from the body and the nervous system. When you express yourself and when you create, you allow yourself to get into and become part of a natural flow, allowing yourself also to connect with the timeless, the magic, that is you. As you allow yourself free expression, every atom in your body and mind is released into a free-flow motion. In turn you open the windows of your mind and consciousness leading to the awareness that you are flowing, moving, and expanding in all directions. Some other keys that you can use to release this magic within yourself are writing, music, drawing, any movement of the body—Tai Chi is excellent— throwing paint on paper, or making love.

Routine, and even what might seem boring tasks, do not have to create suppression and boredom. You can mentally resolve to carry out even these mundane tasks in a conscious joyful way. Bring consciousness, joy and awareness into all that you do and there will not be boredom, a feeling of being "stuck," or suppression leading to stress. Because the every-day is where we often do get stuck, the mind looks at a known task or experience and a little voice in our head says: "This is not going to be fun, I have done it a hundred times. I do not want to do it. It's going to be boring. There is noth-ing new to be gained from it." You have the choice to tell that little voice: "I am not going to accept that, I will be open to seeing, doing, and experiencing the event or task in every possible way." You will notice then that there are many new perspectives and happenings in what you thought you already knew so well. Then the task isn't boring after all. So making a change in how you decide to perceive events allows you to view events in an open and new way.

Stress can be seen then not as doing too much but in not allowing ourselves enough self-expression and openness to enjoy whatever we do. It is not that life is not wonderful; we are just not allowing ourselves to see, experience and be the "wonderful" in all of it. We anaesthetize ourselves by choos-ing and living the reality of the "bored" one instead of seeing and experiencing life in all the other ways it can be, and then choosing to live it differently. Anaesthetizing ourselves is another reason why people overeat and are overweight, or overindulge in alcohol and drugs. This allows them to sup-press themselves and not make enough opportunities for creativity or self-expression. People who feel their lives are boring and empty do not accept that their lives are their own creations. I heard one wise mother say to a child when he complained that everything was boring: "Well, stop being boring then!"

When you are stressed, you often do not feel like making an effort to make love, to express yourself sexually, or to do any of the many other things that would bring release. To stop yourself from further feeling as if you are out of touch and on automatic, it is good at such times to make an effort to touch, to be touched, to move around physically, to do anything which helps you return to your natural state of self-expression, release and balance. Passion, and intensity of emotion in any form, acts as a fire to ignite the mind and the senses, releasing the magic that we are but have suppressed deep within. Remember, magic does not have to remain deep within or hidden. So when you feel stuck, stressed or bored, making the effort is a key to changing this reality. Take a walk, stretch the body, do some deep breathing, let out a long scream, but do not allow yourself to believe that you are a prisoner of your own negative feelings, because with a little effort, you can change the reality and move on to the next new and exciting moment.

Rebirthing

There is always much you can do alone and you will find more and more of your own ways. If you feel that you do need support and help to let go, there are numerous options available. With any counseling or therapy it is important to choose to work with someone you like and feel good with, a person you can feel safe with, open up to, and be yourself with. Counseling can be a lengthy process; you may feel that you want to move through past issues and strong emotional blocks faster. Investigate your options. Ask questions. Feel comfortable about the level of understanding you have regarding how the sessions work and have an idea of what to expect.

Two of the therapies that I use and highly recommend are Rebirthing and Regression therapy.

Rebirthing works primarily with the emotions and the physical body; although the mind in many ways is a large part of the rebirthing process. Some of the clients I rebirth have been involved in counseling for many years and are still looking for answers, solutions and release. Although counseling can be most helpful, there comes a point where even though you can understand all of your issues, letting go of the pain needs something that will work on a much deeper level.

Other rebirthing clients have done little or no other work on themselves and rebirthing works wonderfully for them too. Occasionally, for certain individuals who have very logical or analytical minds, it may not be initially easy to accept the concept of rebirthing and letting go. It can be easy for such people to tie themselves up in concepts, endless statements made in books by others on rebirthing, and to become entangled in complex self-analysis. When such people are ready to move on, they too can stop, take a deep breath and allow themselves the release that rebirthing initiates.

I recommend working with a rebirther who does not spread sessions over long periods of time. One or two sessions is really enough. Working over many sessions is not the best option because only a certain amount of release work is done in each session. The client is then left on his or her own to deal with whatever is taking place, until the next session.

Group rebirthing is also available. Although group rebirthing can be of some benefit, the participant cannot receive the individual attention needed from the rebirther when so many participants are rebirthing at the same time.

A rebirther who is also a sensitive is a bonus, as this person will not only be following known rebirthing techniques, but will have a real sense of what to do for you and when.

Rebirthing is about connected breathing. The basis is that we breathe in life "the new," the everything we need, and we breathe out and release everything we no longer need. There are different stages of the rebirthing; it can be a wonderfully powerful, even moving experience. The individual will discover once again his or her own natural breathing rhythms, and at some point, some people may cry or express rage. Others will not. Rebirthing is as individual as the people who experience the session. But after a session it is common to feel very positive, energized, free, or very light. You may feel that the weight that you have been carrying forever is finally gone.

Therapists will each have their own ways of conducting a session. To give an example, I use a small, comfortable warm room. I use soft lighting and gentle background music. The client lies on the floor cocooned in quilts, covers, and soft pillows. The idea is to create a warm, safe, comfortable space rather like the womb. I get back with clients seven to ten days after the session to follow up and see how and where they are within themselves, as the process needs at least this amount of time before checking results. Again and again clients tell me how rebirthing changed their lives in the most amazingly positive ways, so this is a therapy I highly recommend. The name "rebirthing" brings with it the sense of being reborn and this is very much the case during and after the process.

Regression

Regression, although useful and helpful to the body and emotions, is understood to work primarily with the mind and psyche. Contrary to the beliefs of many people, the regression state does not need to be induced by hypnosis. It is achieved by entering a state of deep relaxation. I always feel good about offering regression in this way without hypnosis, because individuals stay conscious of everything that is happening both in past regression time and in present time, and they make their own conscious choices throughout the session by following their own feelings. The technique I developed is simple and will be introduced in a forthcoming book so that everyone can integrate it into their own self-healing session when needed.

Some professionals are now offering regression as a

therapy. This is preferable to those who offer it simply as a straightforward experience. For instance, if you find yourself going back to a childhood experience where you were unhappy, lonely or unloved, you need to do more than simply view, feel and accept the situation. A regression therapist who uses regression as a healing modality will help you understand that this is your reality and in this moment you can choose to make happen whatever you feel. The idea then is not to think, but to feel what you really want to happen or to do in that moment. You might feel like walking away from events, or being hugged, or saying what you really feel, even confronting those around you. Then you get to act out the past experience in a positive and healing way. This is a lifeline for those who have been abused in childhood particularly because it gives back to the child the power that was taken from him or her in the past situation. It also gives the power to confront the past abuse in a safe, positive and empowered way. The next step is that you take time to feel the good, positive feelings of control and relief you receive by your actions. You feel good then, and stay with these feelings for a few minutes, breathing them deeply throughout your body. By going through this process you have literally changed the past and healed that part of you that was scared and brutalized. This will clear many negative thoughts and behavioral patterns that you have been experiencing in the "here and now" stemming from the past.

Regression and rebirthing are both powerful tools to work with for deep release issues. The great news is that whatever you have suffered and endured in the past, you do not need to be stuck with the pain and negative patterns and blocks. There is much you can do alone and much you can do with help.

Letting go happens on many levels in many ways. We each have our own paths and our own needs. Strong emotions, even hate, can be cleared and let go of in your life.

Perhaps hate has been or is a consuming part of your existence. You will have your own reasons and have made your
choice to hate at some point whether you realize this or not.
When you feel tired of this emotion or drained by it, know
that you can let it go just like all other emotions. As you
move forward with your life, you will find that it becomes
easier to have perspective on why you chose to experience
what might seem to others or even to yourself later such an
extreme emotion.

Chapter 8

What to Do

꿍

We have looked at many different aspects of illness, imbalance and self-healing as a natural process. Let's now get down to the basics and see what to do during your own healing sessions.

The Healing Session

Welcome to your own self-healing experience and the exciting discoveries that await you, the healer! Remember that, although I am using minor aliments and illnesses as examples, self-healing can be used for any health condition. The session can be as described below or include any of the exercises presented in chapter 9.

Let's take the example of a recurring pain on which you need to work over a period of time, perhaps a few days or longer. Let's say that your foot, arm or stomach is giving you a problem.

Preparing Yourself

Prepare yourself to clear the situation and pain by the use of positive thoughts and complete commitment within yourself to heal. Find a time when you can be relaxed and work on the problem area. It could be once a day or a few times a day, whichever you feel is best and decide to make time for. Take off any watches, rings and jewelry before you begin. Now decide that enough is enough of this present situation and pain, and use positive affirmations such as: "I am of pure light and pure energy"; "I am letting go of everything I no longer need"; "I am ready for positive change"; "My body heals and balances itself."

Getting to the root

Begin by getting to the root of the problem and asking yourself: "What is the problem really about? Why do I have this situation?" You will see in the next section how to get your own answers to these questions. Recognize what is going on with you and your body, and commit yourself to taking action to bring change. Fulfill any needs you have, even in small ways if you cannot fulfill the bigger ones. Ask yourself also: "What is this situation of pain and imbalance bringing me? What are the positives? Am I giving myself attention or time by having pain or being ill?" Realize and work with these answers too. Take action if appropriate. Do not allow yourself to believe that you do not know, cannot see or go beyond, even if the answers do not come to you immediately. Write things down if this helps. Your answers may be straightforward or may be obscured among other answers. Keep going and deal with each piece at a time. You may be someone who can do this very fast. The process itself is very fast. If it is very slow for you, realize that you are beginning a different way of thinking, doing and being with which you are perhaps not familiar. So just take your time. You will get there eventually and you will find that your answers become easier to access with each scenario. Go with what you feel rather than relying only on logic. Examine the facts of what has and is happening. Do not disregard thoughts and feelings until you feel confident you have examined them. Reaching conclusions will often take the form of "knowing" within you, even if you cannot explain to yourself the "knowing" itself. The important point is to find out why you have illness, imbalance or pain in your body.

By going through this process you may find that you have already cleared your physical pain or imbalance. Recognition of your needs is sometimes enough by itself to balance the physical body. If you feel you have a situation that requires a deeper letting go and healing, turn to self-expression. Any of the letting go techniques mentioned in the previous chapter such as Rebirthing and Regression will be helpful for the physical, mental, emotional and spiritual parts of yourself.

Color and visualization

If you feel you do not need that level of healing and letting go, continue with your own self-healing by opening up and directing energy to specific parts of your physical body. To do this, visualize the area you are working on being surrounded by color. Choose a color that feels good for you, perhaps a warm orange, yellow, electric blue, purple or green. To choose a color, feel a range of colors and decide which one feels the most powerful, energizing, soothing or calming for you. Imagine your foot, for example, being surrounded and enveloped by this color, not only from the outside of the body but also from the inside. Imagine the color also nurturing and loving this particular area.

Healing with the hands

Now rub the palms of your hands together for a few moments until they both feel warm and alive and you feel connected to them. If you hold your palms a few inches apart in front of yourself now for a few minutes, you may feel a subtle energy between them, rather like two magnets. Some people feel warmth, others cold. Play with this feeling and enjoy it for a while. If you are not aware of this subtle energy, just continue anyway because it will be there at some point during one of your sessions. Now place your hands on the part of your body where you visualized the color. You can place the hands separately, side by side, or one on top of the other. Initially it might feel easier to concentrate on having the palm centered on the area rather than relying too much on the fingertips. Keep your hands touching the area of your body that needs healing for as long as you feel you need to, maybe a few minutes or as many as ten. While you are doing this, you can have the thought from time to time that you are open to healing energy, the "all that is" which surrounds us all and fills this planet and the universe, and that you are a part of the "all that is," not only open to it but allowing yourself to become it. See yourself as becoming expanded, as big as you wish. You could also place a crystal on the area of your body and place one or both hands on top of it. The amount of energy open to you is limitless and goes on forever.

Note that I use the word "energy" because at this time, we have not yet clearly defined what this nonphysical matter exactly is or even what we are, although scientific terms are used and scientific explanations are offered. So if thinking in terms of "energy" works for you, that is fine.

Ending the session

When you have finished, relax for a few minutes. Some people like to wash their hands after a session. Do whatever feels right for you. If you work on someone else, it is a good idea to wash your hands after a session as it allows you time to regroup, to reconnect with you and cut yourself off from the other person. Then you do not find yourself empathizing, feeling their emotions or pain. While you are healing with your hands, you may become aware of different colors or sparks of energy coming from one or both hands. You may feel a warmth or cold feeling flowing through your hands as you place them on yourself or on the other person. When you are healing yourself or others, open yourself up, relax and have the intention of healing energy itself being directed at the part of your body that needs the attention. Believe the healing process to be simple and possible, as it is.

Use these directions as an outline but allow yourself to find your own way. Do whatever comes to you. Do not allow yourself to rush or panic, or feel that you do not know what to do next. Trust yourself. The healing process happens naturally. The intensity and physical sensations felt during a healing session will be different for everyone, although there will be some similarities in these experiences too. You can accept the process of healing as it is happening, and you can also direct your focus and your intention to heal through your hands with your mind. There will be a point when you strongly feel energy, warmth and even denseness in your hands. You have the choice to keep the process as simple or as complex as you wish. Practice. Be aware of any feelings or changes no matter how big or small they may be, and do give yourself time. Do not necessarily expect visible results in one day, but know that what you are doing is always bringing healing on some level. At the same time, be open to the possibility of something amazing happening, and it will, if your intent is strong enough. If you work on someone else, there is no reason why you should feel drained afterwards. Let yourself relax and regroup, and with your thoughts draw to yourself once again all that you need, recharging yourself if you do feel depleted in some way with the following thought in mind: "I draw to myself all that I need."

Whatever part of your body is hurting, deal with it. Touch it. Love it. Ask this part what it wants and needs. It is quite amazing when you watch how people who are hurting, and out of touch with their bodies, will act. They will talk about and allow the hurting part to be displayed to the healer or the physician, but they continue to peer at this part cautiously, talking about it in disconnected terms, as if they are waiting for someone else to touch it, take over and heal it for them. It is almost as if this part of their body is alien to them. These persons are simply not realizing that they can get involved and heal themselves. They are holding themselves back. So stay in touch with even those places that hurt or don't look good. Don't isolate them. They are yours.

How to see, feel and find your own answers

Finding out why you are ill, having pain and various ailments is a matter of asking yourself why and believing in your own answers. For some, the question will be asked and the answer will be there simply and immediately. For others, it will take further commitment. Let's look at how the answers might appear to you.

For example, you might ask: "Why do I have no energy and a pain in my chest?" Wait for the answer. It might come to you as a thought: "It's because you are not being good to yourself," or "You need some time for yourself," or "You are distressed and are reacting about your husband's work situation," or "It's because you need to tell your mother how you really feel about coming to visit," or "You don't feel you are being treated fairly at work," or "You don't feel your girlfriend is being truthful," or any one of a billion other reasons.

The answer might come to you in a picture: "you are running away chased by someone or chased by events," or "you are feeling as if you are very small and insecure and the world is very big and overpowering." You might see a picture of strawberries or bacon. If you do, the next question will be: "Do I need the strawberries or bacon or should I stop eating them?" Then perhaps, "Do I need more fruit and vegetables in my diet, or animal protein, or should I stop eating meat?" Follow your answers through. If you see yourself being chased by many people, ask yourself what does this remind you of in your life, who do you feel is chasing you, hounding you or putting pressure on you? Is it a person, several people, an organization or a certain situation?

You might also receive the answer to your question not as a thought but a feeling, perhaps sadness or misery, pain, anxiety, fear or loneliness. Feel this feeling and then take your question to the next level by asking yourself what is making you feel this emotion. Is it people or situations you are in now? Are you making yourself feel this way because of something you have or have not done? How long have you felt this emotion? Is it from present time, recent time, or does it go back as far as you can remember? Where does this emotion come from? What happened or what were the events and circumstances in general that made you feel this way? It may help if you write your answers down. Sometimes it may seem like a puzzle, and the pieces are revealed and can be fitted into place one at a time.

You may not get a thought, a picture, or a scene in your mind, or even an emotional feeling. Instead you might feel compelled to stop what you are doing and do something else, call someone you have not spoken to for a while, read a page of a book again that you had put to one side, walk or drive to a certain place for no reason other than you feel you need to be there. Go ahead, forget logic and do whatever you feel compelled to do.

Lots of different possibilities exist concerning how you will find your own answers to your initial question. We can call them triggers. They are a part of a jigsaw puzzle and may bring to you missing pieces. Then you can put them into place. Sometimes we ask ourselves questions and then later—minutes, hours or days, even weeks—someone else answers them for us. Sometimes you hear the answer on the radio or television or read it in the newspaper or a book. Synchronicity comes into play here. We create ways of finding our own answers, often without realizing that we created them. Some people find answers in words, others in symbols. But remember, you are working with your own mind and you will never receive an answer to your questions that you cannot understand by yourself. The more you practice asking and answering your own questions, the easier it will become because you will gain experience of how your mind works.

You are also quite capable of seeing your body both inside and out, and the blocks of other people. This is an ability that you may have used before or possibly did not even think you had. But you can do this too; it only takes self-belief and practice. Self-belief in this instance mainly means saying no to everything that is inside your mind telling you that it is not possible, or that you don't know how.

For example, you have had a pain in your elbow for a while or maybe it just started. Sit or stand comfortably. Hold the elbow with the other hand, placing your palm or fingertips on the painful area. Have your eyes open and look directly at your elbow. Feel it, decide you are going to look at how it looks inside. You may physically see how it looks in a very basic medical way, seeing the muscles, flesh tissue, blood vessels and bones. You may see an inflammation, a redness or sore-looking part. You may even receive feelings and thoughts that go with this picture: my elbow is painful because there is an inflammation and it is bruised; or perhaps there may be some other feelings and thoughts.

Instead of keeping your eyes open, you may want to close them, hold the elbow with your other hand, touch it, caress it or not hold it at all. Once again, decide that you want to see how it looks inside. This time you might receive a mental image in your mind, not necessarily of how it looks from a medical point of view. Instead you might see the area being surrounded by a shadow or a color, you might see something which seems to be totally unrelated, such as a cartoon character or something else which seems ridiculous. Accept this image and then decide to move forward. It is quite usual when you first look "clairvoyantly" or "clearly" to see cartoon characters or other images that seem ridiculous. This is the part of you and your mind that tries to throw you off track by saying: "This is ridiculous!" But persevere, because that is not all you are capable of seeing.

Each person will see clairvoyantly a little differently from another. It really does not matter how you see or how you get your answers. There is not a right or wrong, good or bad way of doing this. Practice, know that you can do it and accept what you see, no matter how small, how ridiculous or amazing it is. Once you get used to looking and seeing, then you can begin to use your feelings to decide what is relevant and useful in what you are seeing. How we see and perceive in many ways is connected initially to how we think. However, we can transcend our thinking and see more clearly what really is. Remember that you can find the answers to the questions you need answered in your self-healing process by allowing thoughts to come, by looking and by feeling.

Say no more!
When you have been through a "letting go" and healing process, do not just hope or wish that this is the end of the pain and the problem. Instead, when you are sure that you have reached the end and that there is nothing more to take

into account, make a firm decision in the form of a statement inside of your mind and self that there will be no more reoccurrence of any related problem. Decide that this is really the end of that past problem and imbalance.

To do this, you may simply imagine that part of yourself being cleared forever. You may think about solid steel doors behind you, or throw away past events far into deep space with the recommendation from your mind that these past events and pains can never come back, or at the very least, not for 70 trillion light years. These are just words I am using to make a point. They might be helpful, but make up your own, find what feels final to you. Do not allow the possibility of reoccurrence of problems to be a reality in your mind. This is merely a way to cover all areas, angles, eventualities and tracks. It's also important not to say, even though it is easy to do so, "Yes, here I am, perfectly well and healthy, but..." That "but" is just an invitation for something to go wrong. Be demanding of yourself and what you want. Do not allow compromise in any way at all. Say: "No more pain!" and really mean "no more." As you gain more practice, you will find that your thoughts and willpower become more focused and more powerful, and when you say "No more," it will be so.

How to heal your past

We looked in the previous chapter at clearing and healing your past with the use of Regression therapy. However, you may not have access to a Regression therapist, or you may not wish to use Regression as a tool. Let's have a look at some exercises that you can use to heal the past. Tools that are instantly accessible to you include visualization, positive thought, pen and paper. Healing the past and letting go can be experienced in many forms and carried out in different ways. The basic idea of healing and clearing will involve visualizing positives where negatives have been, saying no to pain or abuse on any level and allowing "you" to be the winner, rather than the victim.

If at any time you feel emotional or physical pain in your body while you are doing past healing and release work, use the combing technique described in chapter 9, or use your hands to nurture, sooth and heal this hurting part of "you." When you are ready, decide that you do not accept pain anymore and allow it to go.

You might have realized, during your self-healing process, that you are still strongly tied to a previous relationship, perhaps even an abusive one, or to a specific event or place. You find yourself still acting out negative patterns, and reacting from past associations. If you decide that you need distance or severance, for example, from a past relationship, begin by removing your watch, jewelry and shoes, and loosen any restrictive clothing. Lie back comfortably. Take long, slow, deep breaths and allow your body to completely relax. Allow a few flashes, pictures of the person you wish to disconnect from, to come into your mind. You may see yourself pictured with this person or separately. First, bring distance between you by imagining both of you in separate spaces. Work on one picture at a time. See this person standing in a large wide-open empty space surrounded with bright yellow, gold or white light, looking well and happy. Now say goodbye to him or her. Decide that this is final. Next, move on to the picture of yourself and see yourself also in a large wide-open empty space surrounded with bright color and light. Look at the expression on your face. Visualize it as a positive and happy one. Do whatever is needed. For example, there might be something you feel that the person needs before you disconnect completely. If so, imagine the person having it. There might be something you need before you can have that happy expression. Visualize yourself having whatever you need too. When you have decided your work is done, you have completed the exercise. Some people like to visualize cords running between themselves and the person they want to distance or disconnect themselves from. Use this visualization if it feels right for you. But, please, know that this is not necessarily how things are. Take your time and cut the cords between you and the person either mentally with just a thought, or by imagining that you are using a bright shiny silver or gold pair of scissors. Have the following thought clearly in your mind at the same time: "I am letting go of everything I no longer need." If you are having a mental picture of the person not willing to let you go, or you do not feel strong enough, doubting that you can do this, stop for a moment. Take a deep breath, and be very clear with yourself that this is your reality, and that no objection can be greater than your will and your mind. Believe in you.

To make the process more final, some people like to dispose of old photographs or possessions belonging to someone that they want to be disconnected from. If you choose to do this, I suggest preparing yourself first emotionally and mentally for a state of positive change. Then, dispose of the photographs or other possessions with the thought in your mind: "I am letting go now of everything I no longer need." Some believe that fire is a great cleanser and are intuitively drawn to burn unwanted possessions. If you can safely do this and it feels right for you, do so. An appropriate trash area outside and away from your house may also be your choice. If you want to sell or give away items belonging to a person you wish to disconnect from, do so thoughtfully, as you will not wish to give to others items that have a lot of negative thoughts and feelings associated with them. You can clean the items before parting from them by piling them together and then visualizing them being cleansed, simply by using your mind to flood them with fire or bright light.

Another exercise to let go and heal the past is using pen and paper. Sit down and write about past events that you feel stuck on or held by. Pour out all of your thoughts and feelings on to the paper. Express yourself in any way that feels right for you. Don't hold back. It's all right to express how you feel. When you have finished, and are ready to release the past events, people and places from your mind, body and being, be clear that the end is now, and that you will not spend any more time or energy getting caught up in negative past events. Make a mental note to absorb any positives that exist in these past experiences, even if you do not quickly see them. Then decide to let go now of all you no longer need. You can dispose of your writings by whichever means that seem more final for you, tearing them into pieces or simply placing them in a trash can outside of your house.

We have looked previously at giving yourself what you need. When healing the past, giving yourself what you need will be both useful and relevant. For example, the small child that was once you and that you can see in your mind, or feel in your heart, may feel sad, confused, alone or afraid. In this case, mentally wrap this child in a warm, soothing cloak of love and nurture him or her. Mentally hold and hug this smaller "you." Ask the child what he or she needs. Then visualize the child receiving and accepting what was missing before. It may not be only the small child in you that needs to be healed, but any and every other "you" along the way. There can be a part of you that needs comfort, love, care, recognition or even simply to be heard. Work with these images as they come up in your life. If you have past events that you wish you had lived differently, act them out differently in your mind. Make them as whole and as positive as you wish. Then, breathe through your body and being the relief that you feel, and the freedom you finally give to yourself by taking these simple actions. Allow yourself to feel good now as you re-enact positively any situation despite how it was played out before. If you have loved ones who have passed on, and feel you never had the chance to say goodbye, or how you felt, or what was on your mind, you can take action and do so now. A photograph or something that belonged to the person can be useful for you to feel connected with that person once again. But if you have nothing, just concentrate with your mind on the person's name and have a mental picture of him or her. That connection can also be strong enough. Now, with your mind, or even with your voice, say all that you need to say. It is never too late. Let go what is in your mind and your heart. Time and space have no distance between us and the ones we love, and those who we have been connected to even in small ways.

For some people, using these techniques will be straight-forward and simple. For others, at times, it will seem as if there is always something else to clear. We are each different. Remember not to push yourself too hard, and don't compare yourself with anyone. Know that you are always progressing, and that at some point your self-healing process will come to an end. Sometimes, the mind and emotions will throw up many minor hurts, fears, pains and anger. If you feel that you have dealt with your larger issues and that these small points are not truly affecting or bothering you, then you can say "enough" to them. Or you can deal with them with just a bright, healing, positive thought such as: "I love myself completely without conditions," or "I am of pure light and energy."

I mention these very small points that may come up because sometimes the mind and emotions might be locked onto bringing up every pain you ever experienced, in areas such as abandonment, loss, insecurity, etc. You do not have to focus on every pain that you have ever felt, but rather the ones that have hurt and continue to hurt you. All the small ones will then be taken care of, as they are mirrors, frag-mentations, and reflections of the larger primary issues.

Allow yourself to heal your past whenever you have the need. It does not have to be only during sessions, and you do not always have to be in a deeply relaxed state. The healing might happen while you are working, eating, sleeping or doing any number of other everyday things. Often a thought, a quick visualization, will be all that is needed in that present moment. Use your own creativity and imagination as you heal your past. Give yourself now, what you never had. Allow to happen what never did. Be open to being all that you are. Remember, you can and will make all of the difference.

The healing room vs. the sick room

Picture for a moment two very different settings. In the first, the individual is surrounded by a warm comfortable ambience. Flowers are placed where they can be noticed. They are colorful and pleasing to the eye. The flowers bring with them beauty and a sense of newness, hope and growth. There is space around the bed or couch where the individual is comfortably resting. Magazines, papers, and reading materials are available, but they are not in the way or in a messy heap. There might be a soothing and beautiful picture on the wall, a peaceful natural scene. The room is filled with natural light coming from a window or windows. Windows can be opened to allow fresh air to circulate throughout the room. There could be soft music playing gently in the background. A very light, delicate scent pleasing to the senses pervades the atmosphere. Any machinery necessary for the patient is stored away when not in use. Medications are not in view but stored until they are needed. The room is filled with a sense of peace, positivity and openness. At night, when there is no natural lighting, soft and warm artificial light is available. The room might be painted a soft pastel color or a warm rich vibrant tone. Something special belonging to the individual is nearby. This could be a photograph, a cuddly toy, something that is brought into the healing room which helps the patient to feel at home and calm. There is no television set.

Now let's look at a different setting. The individual rests
on an unmade bed or couch. There is clutter everywhere.
Fruit, which is no longer fresh, is in view. Unwashed glasses
and food trays are around the room. Reading materials lie in
a heap. The room is either dark or bright white and entirely
sterile. There is a smell of antiseptic and medication. The
temperature is either too hot or too cold. The atmosphere
feels alien. A constant noise in the background, unknown
voices, and machinery pervade the ambience. Medication is
piled high on the nightstand. The room has little or no natural light or air; the room itself is small or cramped. Nothing
here feels good.

These two different settings could be in a hospital, a
nursing home, or even at the individual's home. The first we
might call a healing room, the second a sick room. It is obvious which one will create a more beneficial healing
environment.

If you are in or have a loved one in the second setting, do
whatever you can to bring light, air and space into the situation and healing space. What you can do physically,
especially in a hospital isolation or intensive care unit, may
seem quite small. But if the room is cramped, do what you can
to create more space. You can even do this by visualizing the
room expanding and being flooded with bright color and
light. Bring in color and light, somehow; doing it even in a
small way will help. Whatever type of room you are confined
in for any period of time during the healing process, make it
as comfortable and cheerful as possible. If you are unable to
move around and do this yourself, ask somebody else to do it
for you. Turn off the television. This applies if you are in hospital or at home. Allow yourself time to let your mind and
body catch up with each other. This is part of the healing
process, whether you have a cold or a minor illness or are in
great pain or discomfort. Allow yourself to be quiet and to
accept the fact that for now you are out of action. Know that

you will get well and that your life and the lives of others are not going to collapse because you need time out right now. Allow yourself to be cared for by others, let go of being in charge. During this time you have an opportunity for much personal expansion and growth. You have chosen to be in this situation and to take this opportunity whether you realize it or not. It makes sense to stop fighting and to go with the flow, not just to heal but also to allow yourself the opportunity to let thoughts and realizations occur to you. There are many ways of living and being other than the functional, which is the way that we all know so well. Often we become afraid to just sit back and allow ourselves to discover this fact. Taking and allowing the time for yourself is a major part of healing; otherwise, you will be fighting yourself and prolonging the healing process. So take the time that you need to heal and also take the time to be unwell. You chose the situation, so explore it.

Visitors to the healing room, besides whatever else they bring, bring above all, themselves. So when you visit, see it as a healing room rather than a sick room. This does not mean being overly positive and cheerful if inside you are full of pain and fear about the one you are visiting. Instead deal with these issues within yourself first, before you visit. Also know that you will have an effect on the person you are visiting. So decide to make it a positive one, but also be aware that your idea of positive may not be what is needed, so don't try too hard to be anything. Rather, be yourself as naturally and fluently and as "you" as possible. The person who is ill will automatically take what they need from you, so there is no need to try and push too hard. Just keep in mind that you are visiting a healing room where wonderful things are possible, and can happen. Expect them too.

When you are sick, allow yourself to have what you need. If you feel like curling up in a ball and hugging a pillow or a soft toy, or being quiet and drifting in and out of sleep states, do it and enjoy the sensations. Let yourself go. Nurture yourself in other ways too. Eat what you want to eat. Your body will tell you what you need, so listen to it. If you feel like being indulgent, do so. Cover yourself with soft clothing, things that make you feel good. If there is someone around who offers to pamper you, let him or her. Allow yourself to daydream. Let your imagination and fantasies run wild, because this might be exactly just what you need. Imagine soft pillows, comfortable sheets. If you have to stay in bed, let it be your healing space, a comfortable cocoon. Even if the space that you are confined to is very small, use your imagination to expand it. Imagine the sounds of gentle running water in the background, birds softly singing harmonious beautiful music in the distance, even a deserted island with only the sounds of the waves gently lapping at the shore. Perhaps you might imagine a beautiful garden filled with every imaginable flower in bloom, beautiful colors and fragrances filling the space, or perhaps simply wide open empty space. Imagine so much room and space that you feel as if you could expand into forever. If you find yourself in a sick room rather than a healing room, make the switch in your mind and bring the kind of space that you or others will best heal in. Imagine lying in the sun and being warmed and fed by its colorful rays.

Do you remember something from when you were a child that helped you to heal? I have a favorite one. When I was a small girl, if I was sick, my mother used to put cake in a dish, sprinkle a little sugar over it, and then cover it with either warm or cold milk. I used to mash it all up and eat it with a very small spoon. It tasted really, really good. This always helped me feel better. It was my way of being pampered and indulgent and it made me feel rich. It was a small thing but it worked.

Recently, I asked a group of people about the small or big things they do when they get sick, what kind of healing space they like or need, and what works best for them during these times of being out of balance. Bret said he rarely gets sick, but if he did, he would like the caring attention of a loving woman around him, as he remembers how well his own mother always looked after him and his sister. He added that good old-fashioned love helped cure many ailments. He would also like to be surrounded by what he calls the colors of life—yellow and green. A woman named Lee said: "I remain in bed under the covers, drink water and herbal tea. No noise and lots of sleep." She added: "My own bedroom is the best healing space for me. It has Windsor green walls and is covered with pictures depicting happy scenes." She also recommends lots of flowers and lots of large pillows. Patricia had simple answers: "Plenty of quiet and rest, understanding from the family, especially children." Donna replied: "My ideal healing space is a clean room without any clutter." She is sure that this allows the mind to relax. Jane does not like any form of sick room but prefers to lie on the sofa and sleep. Sometimes she goes out into the garden and listens to the birds, which calms her down and makes her forget about feeling bad. Finally Jane says: "I ask for lots of hugs from my boys and drink hot tea." Raul wrote simply: "I offer no resistance to illness. I go with the flow. I flood myself with bright white light and head outside to be by a stream or in a forest." Solitude and the harmony within nature works for him. Another lady, whose name is Sophie said: "I always lie down and get plenty of sleep. I don't like bright light. I change my bedroom around by simply pulling my bed away from the walls and placing it in the middle of the room, so that I can allow healing energies to move around the room."

These people are not necessarily acting on what they have been told, but on what they feel themselves, what they have tried and tested, and found to be effective for them. We will each have our own ways of doing things, but obviously it pays to take control. Go with the flow of your own feelings.

Treat sickness and the healing room with the individualism and imagination that is yours. It would seem that often, when we are sick, we are stopped in our tracks and forced to take a moment to focus on ourselves. Illness offers for many of us a rare opportunity to be in touch with ourselves and to ask, What do I really need right now, at this time? Allow yourself to explore illness and imbalance within your own comfortable boundaries. Treat it without fear, recognize the positives as well as the negatives of the experience and get to know yourself and how you work even better during the process.

Food, shape and balance

With all the books and products now available for weight loss, and the huge amount of diet products and food supplements on the supermarket shelves, it's interesting to note that for the first time in history, there are, since 1998, more overweight people in the United States than people who are not. An article published in Natural Health magazine (March 2000) stated that "fifty-four percent of adult Americans are overweight, according to the National Center for Health Statistics". Newsweek, in an article titled "Generation XXL", published on July 3, 2000, reported that "by the government's estimate, some 6 million American children are now fat enough to endanger their health. An additional 5 million are on the threshold, and the problem is growing more extreme even as it becomes more widespread." Holding on to weight and being out of shape does not seem then to be only about food.

Most of us have an idea of what feels a comfortable weight and shape for our bodies. This often happens when we reach the point of accepting and liking ourselves, and no longer striving for the super-thin athletic shapes and so-called "perfect" images we are constantly bombarded with in magazines and television. There are people who eat whatever they want and stay in great shape. But looking more closely at these people, they generally have busy lives and often a good positive mental attitude. Eating in moderation will be for many people a big part of staying in balance, but remember that your state of mind does make a difference. Thoughts are powerful. If you believe you're going to put on weight if you eat candy bars, you probably will. One of the most positive thoughts to start developing is an idea of being in perfect weight and shape and staying that way whatever you eat. It's as simple as that. Take control, make up your mind and you will create that reality.

If you are very overweight, not by the perfect standards but your own standard, you will need to be really honest with yourself. You may feel fine about being overweight and like yourself just as you are. That is all right too, if you are truly happy with your body. However, if you feel out of control with your situation, then it is important to begin making time for yourself and to examine what's going on. Start by asking yourself: "Why am I overweight?" Each person will have his or her own reasons. You may see that you feel stressed, have no time for yourself, feel like a failure, unloved, unappreciated, angry, not good enough, or perhaps you may feel a sense of loneliness or loss. Maybe you use food as a way to let go or to feel good for a while.

Relationships and work situations are also often connected to weight gain: unhappy relationships, fear of expressing yourself or of losing that relationship. We see people who are alone wondering when that someone special will be coming into their lives, while they are still hurting over previous relationships, sometimes ones in the distant past. Although these people may wish for someone new, they allow themselves to be overweight and decide they are unattractive. As a result, they keep others at a distance, not allowing themselves to become involved or hurt again. It seems that they try to keep their distance from life itself. Simply, these people are just not ready for a new relationship. There is nothing wrong with being not ready. Sometimes, it might be interesting, even fascinating, not to be in the dating game for a while. It's one way of taking time out, even getting to know yourself, to realize all over again that being attractive to yourself may well be a key factor in being attractive to others.

Boredom is another reason often cited for being overweight or out of shape. Does anyone ever consider what being bored really means? I have delved into this matter and seen that boredom occurs when you are full, to the point of having no room left for anything new to stimulate or excite you on any level, physical, emotional or intellectual. We've become so full of old thoughts and experiences and ways that there is no room to see anything in a new light or from a new perspective. Boredom does not have to mean that you are stuck. This is an assumption. In fact, there is a part of boredom that allows one to be still. So even if being bored looks negative, it might have its own great purpose, giving you another option and way of being. To be miserable sometimes is all right too, and is needed sometimes as well. We have constant choices and even negative ones are not necessarily bad. Each choice takes us to different experiences, realities and realizations within ourselves. After all, we have in our life time and space for everything.

Of course, there are known medical reasons why some people are overweight. I find amazing the number of women over forty, for instance, being diagnosed with thyroid imbalance and accepting this as the reason for their weight problem. I am not saying that thyroid problems are not real. However, I have seen countless women in this particular situation who are generally unhappy in their relationships. Children have grown up. They find little or no satisfaction in sex. They wonder who they really are, feeling that they have gotten lost or put to one side during their journey in life. I have seen many cases where these women started examining themselves and their feelings. Then they began to find themselves again and feel good as they worked on the real core issues affecting their lives. Some women may only need to bring small, but effective changes into their lives. For others, the changes may need to be more dramatic. Often after six months, perhaps a year, these same women are back in shape and balance, without thyroid problems or thyroid medication.

Being out of shape does not only refer to being overweight. It can be feeling depressed or lethargic, no longer caring, watching your dreams just slip away, or becoming desensitized. I remember well a man who had become desensitized and had not been able to feel emotionally or physically for many years. This man often felt bored and depressed. It did not matter what he had, nothing brought joy into his life. One day ran into another. He watched others who could derive satisfaction and pleasure from the small simple things in life, but he couldn't. His body and emotions remained frozen. He went on to change that situation, and so can you.

Being out of balance includes conditions such as anorexia and bulimia. Anorexia is to under-eat, starvation being the extreme example. Bulimia is to over-eat, obesity being the extreme of this condition. Forcing food out of the body either through vomiting or with the use of laxatives is common in both conditions. Either condition can be changed if the person decides they want change. Treatment often involves counseling and therapy. In extreme cases, hospitalization may be necessary if the person has gone beyond safephysical limits.

As extreme as these two conditions may be, there is in both an open pathway to explore the self and personality, because at some point both the bulimic and the anorexic have made this personal choice. Again, the first questions to ask are "Why?" and "What is this really all about?" It is advisable to be prepared to ask these questions before the physical, emotional or mental body is adversely affected and damaged by these ways of being. However, even in extreme cases people have and do come back from the brink of self-destruction. The anorexic or bulimic sufferer needs to explore control issues on basic and deeper levels within themselves and their lives. As issues are resolved and the individual feels in control and safe, the focus on food will no longer need to be an issue.

Good food and bad food

We hear constantly about good and bad foods. We've become obsessed with reading food labels. If you ever hear a professional nutritionist speak, you might well come to the conclusion that there is little left on the planet that is safe or good to eat. It is easy to realize that we have at one time or another each bought into this idea, the good food and bad food syndrome, to varying degrees.

The lists of good foods and bad foods are constantly changing. For example, chocolate might taste great but was considered in the past to be bad. Now, however, we are told it can be good for us. When you see how much data is available and realize that evidence can be found both for and against almost everything, it puts the whole matter into perspective.

It is also a little shocking how well media and advertising campaigns work. I was talking recently to a young woman who lives in France and was born in Australia. She asked me about her general health and was concerned about skin problems. She was not on any medication, but listed over thirty different vitamins, food supplements, and proteins she took daily. This is not an unusual case; I see it more and more nowadays. I suggested she cut out all of these alternatives and eat a basic vegetarian diet for a month, with lots of fruits and vegetables, and plenty of room temperature water so her body could detoxify and get back to a more natural state. Then, I suggested that after that she take another look at her situation. She was alarmed and said, "But aren't vitamins supposed to be good for you?" Later this young woman explained that she was afraid of not taking her vitamins. She almost believed that her body would fall apart without them, and that she would possibly be attacked by any germ or virus around her. I reassured her that this would not happen, and she took my advice. After only a few days, she called again and was a great deal calmer. Her skin condition had improved.

Many people are in this same predicament, consuming vast amounts of vitamins, minerals and food supplements, believing that you can't have too much of a good thing. Nancy Deutsch, in an article published by Reuters Health on March 6, 2000, reports that "a toddler with mental retardation who was undergoing an unsupervised megavitamin and megamineral treatment died of magnesium poisoning". Laurie Drake, in another article titled "Too much of a good thing" presents the case of Susan, a 35-year-old accountant, who suffered an overdose of vitamins. "Proving that it's possible to get too much of a good thing, Susan and others like her are a nutritional paradox—healthy people who are getting sick on vitamins. 'Vitamins are medicines like anything else, and in every medicine there is a little poison,' says New York City cardiologist Isadore Rosenfeld, who points out that grossly exceeding recommended daily allowances can lead to everything from nausea, diarrhea and constipation to bone pain and birth defect. But striking the right balance of the 40 essential vitamins and minerals can be tough, since proper dosage varies with a person's age, sex and other factors" (Allure, May 1998). Because of advertising campaigns promoting 100 percent natural products, a lot of people feel reassured by the word "natural." But the point is, whenever you take these products, you are giving your power and belief to a substance outside of yourself and not allowing yourself to discover your own healing thought process and your own body's healing abilities. You are never giving yourself the chance to see that you can function as well, if not better, without such products. Keep in mind that it is easy to become out of touch with your body, your mind and your emotions. Chemical reactions may be so subtle as to go largely unnoticed, but the effects can be quite profound.

Each month, new discoveries are made of foods or drinks linked to a particular illness or a particular cure, with findings on both the positive and the negative poles of the spectrum. The message is clear. It is barely possible to keep up with all this data of good or bad food, but you can always listen to yourself. When you really believe in something, a miracle tablet or plant extract, and use it, it is possible that you lower your defenses and allow your body's own healing process to work. You use the outside source simply as a focus, but it is you who is doing the healing. But if you are not aware of what you are doing and of this process happening, then you may not be aware of just how much healing work you did, and how much the medication or supplement actually worked. So you have once again given away your own self-belief without even thinking about it, simply by listening to convincing ad campaigns and taking facts and figures to be absolute.

It is important in your self-healing and new lifestyle to develop the belief and awareness that you know what is good for you. Your needs and eating habits will of course, also change along the way, even after you feel you have got things exactly right. So don't get stuck in your own regime and patterns either. You can reach a point where you take control of what you eat and consume, based on what you feel, and find a place of balance for yourself, finally free from being blinded and dominated by advertising campaigns. You clearly have the option to enjoy or not to enjoy food in your own particular way.

Nutrition has become in the past few decades such a science and sign of wealth that we appear to have forgotten the simplicity of healthy food, which we used to consume not too long ago. The following anecdote illustrates the fact that we do know, within ourselves, what is good for us to eat. I took a short vacation recently with my husband to the Grand Canyon and Monument Valley on the Utah/Arizona border. We went horseback riding, slept under the stars and stayed in a hogan, the Navajo Indians' authentic house. Our guide, Mike, was a Native American Indian and was a gentle, and pleasant man. He was perhaps one hundred pounds overweight and he expressed his sorrow and concern about it. The Navajo diet seemed to consist of a lot of oily, pan-fried bread, large steaks, and some salad and corn. We noticed most of the Native Indians, men, women and children, were also overweight. Mike noted that we were in good shape and asked us our secret. I told him that we had been vegetarians for years and gave him some basic tips about diet and lifestyle that I felt might be helpful. Then I began to look more closely at him, and saw that he was not happy. I explained that he was carrying a lot of emotional pain from the past that he had to let go. He was divorced, the youngest brother of five, and the least successful brother materially. One brother had over forty horses. Mike had five. He was striving hard to change his position and we discussed his business of working with tourists and how he could improve it. Interestingly enough, this gentle man seemed impressed with our advice, but unsure about the vegetarianism idea. The answer to his doubt came via the local newspaper a few days later, in a fascinating article published in the April 8 issue of the *Navajo Times*: "Traditional Diets Prove More Healthy for Native Americans." It began by pointing out that "if you spend anytime at a reservation clinic, you will find patient after patient with diabetes, cancer and high blood pressure. It wasn't always that way. It need not be that way now. A more traditional diet is the prescription needed to avoid much of that suffering." The article explained that current federal guidelines push a "Westernized" diet that does not take into account the health needs and cultural practices of Native Americans and other minorities. "For Native Americans, current federal dietary guidelines promoting a cheesy, meaty diet amounts to, perhaps inadvertently, the nutritional equivalent of smallpox-infected blankets." The article also stated that Hollywood depicts the Indian as a great hunter, a big meat eater, and killer of buffalo. However this was not actually the case. "In fact, with exceptions such as the Apaches, few tribes, in what is now the United States, hunted much (though some fished) before white people came.... Earlier, vegetables, legumes and whole grains were dietary staples for many tribes. Iroquois, grew seventeen varieties of corn, seven types of squash, and 60 of beans . . . They also gathered a cornucopia of 34 wild fruits, 11 nut species, 12 kinds of edible roots, 38 types of bark, six fungi, and maple syrup." I left the article for Mike to read, wished him well, and hoped his people soon found their way.

I have been a vegetarian for at least half of my life. But it is a personal choice, not an absolute. I believe it is the first basic conscious choice to be made towards wholeness. In western society, vegetarianism makes a lot of sense to me; it feels like a positive choice. There are endless facts and horror stories about the terrible conditions animals are reared in and the horrific circumstances they are butchered and die in. If something dies in pain or fear, I will not bring that flesh into my body and reality. I agree that there was a time when animals lived in harmony with humans and mankind took the being of that animal into their bodies with reverence and awareness. Even now some animals are reared with kindness and killed in humane ways. To eat meat acquired in this way might be an acceptable option.

On an economic level, we are told that if the world became vegetarian, we would have enough space to grow food for the whole world's population. This might be idealistic, but there is something inside of me that wants to be a part someday of that beautiful reality where everybody has food to eat and no one is starving. It almost seems nonsense that it is not already so.

Vegetarianism is much misunderstood by non-vegetarians and even many longtime vegetarians. The fear of not getting enough protein is a classic point and many vegetarians overuse what they consider substitute products such as soy and tofu for meat. I personally rarely eat either of these products and I say that there is no need to substitute anything. Substitution can bring with it the concept that if I don't have a substitute, I am missing out somehow and therefore something bad will happen to me. In a report presenting the position of The American Dietetic Association (ADA) on vegetarian diets, Virginia K. Messina, MPH, RD, and Kenneth I. Burke, PhD, RD, state that "plant sources of protein alone can provide adequate amounts of essential amino acids if a variety of plant foods are consumed and energy needs are met . . . Research suggests that complementary proteins do not need to be consumed at the same time and that consumption of various sources of amino acids over the course of the day should ensure adequate nitrogen retention and use in healthy persons."

Of course, vegetarianism isn't the solution to everything. I have been approached often by overweight, out of shape vegetarians who also have all kinds of problems. So my advice is, vegetarian or not, eat what you feel and always be open to change. Be informed and give new foods a chance. Let your body tell you what it needs. You've probably heard the age-old saying "a little of what you fancy does you good." Moderation is great. It might be perfect for many people. But again, it's not the only way.

Food can be a pleasure to eat, and wonderful to share. We have all enjoyed a pleasant meal with friends or family. It can also be satisfying to cook something tasty for yourself, taking time to make the effort for no one else but you. One of my clients told me what she does occasionally to give herself a treat. She takes a long bath, wears something sensuous, and sets the table for one with attractive china and crystal glassware. Then she takes a long time to cook herself something really special. Next, she sits down to enjoy every mouthful and focuses her thoughts on positive future dreams. She mentioned that she is married, but does not invite her husband to share this special occasion. It is something she prefers and enjoys alone.

There are other people who eat purely to live and are not particularly interested in food, and those who have never really opened themselves to the pleasures of eating. Though it is all right to enjoy food, it's also all right not to enjoy it.

Comfort eating is a pattern most of us have developed at one time or another in our lives. For some, it happens now and again. For others, it's a regular part of life. Interestingly, when we "comfort eat," we tend to choose sweet, soft, creamy rich foods, much like the foods we would have preferred as children. There is a link between the child within us—the emotional, vulnerable part of us—and habits formed in childhood. How many parents give their children something sweet or nice to eat as a treat or as a "pick-me-up" when life is not going just right?

To overindulge in food can be a way of letting go. It can give a sense of freedom. But if your waistband starts becoming tight or if you start becoming very overweight then, perhaps it's time to look again at how you are using food and for what purpose. There are lots of ways to overindulge besides food. Look also at the particular need that encourages you to overindulge. What is it really all about? Enjoy it and overindulge, but don't feel trapped by it. However, if you like feeling trapped, look at that part of yourself too.

Getting back in shape and letting go of painful past emotions can be rather like a toothache you've had for a long time. You get the tooth removed and you are happy that the pain is gone but for a while you almost feel like something is missing. Obviously, the very best thing to do beyond comfort eating would be to stay with the emptiness. Let it envelop you and see what is at the end of it. Once you have come to the end of emptiness, it will never return in the same way and you will have grown in your own awareness and realization. It is important to know that the emptiness you feel, regardless of the circumstances that led you to that way of being, does have an end and you can reach it. I remember a long time ago, I had an experience of the emptiness and the void. It seemed it would last forever. At the time, I did not know what to do. A wise part of me said: "If you don't know what to do, then do nothing, keep going and know that however things seem, the emptiness and nothingness does have an end, just keep moving and traveling through it." Sure enough, that was exactly what happened.

It may be helpful to remind yourself, if you are in that position, that time and space have no distance. You do have enough time and everything that happens along that journey is valuable and relevant. So keep going!

We often eat as a quick way to cope with our emotions, and not necessarily because of a physical need. Next time you feel a hole in your stomach, visualize a color, perhaps yellow, purple or orange and imagine that you are surrounded by that color. Then take deep breaths from the bottom of the stomach, breathing the color all through the body until you feel full and satisfied. People are often surprised that they are no longer hungry. I have a client who skips the occasional meal and breathes deeply the color "yellow" instead. He swears that his emotional center and body are satisfied and that he feels great by breathing color. He says it also keeps him in great shape as he rarely overeats. So this approach does work; it offers an alternative to the comfort eating that might otherwise occur when you feel emotionally empty.

If you feel out of touch with your body and what is good for you to eat, I suggest getting back to the basics and simplicity. Cut out processed foods, excessive amounts of sugar and sweeteners. Cut back on carbonated drinks containing sugar, saccharin or Nutra Sweet, and drink plenty of room temperature water. Include in your diet plenty of grains, fresh fruits and vegetables, rice, pasta and other staples. Try eating small meals and snacks regularly rather than large meals. When you feel hungry, drink a glass of water, take a few deep breaths and then check to see if you are still hungry. When you shop, look around and open yourself to the possibility of trying foods with different colors, flavors and textures than you might normally buy. Include food in your life, but no longer be consumed by constant thoughts of it. Don't try to get things right, rather give yourself what you want and need, and feel good about yourself. After a few short weeks, you will find yourself back in touch with your body and emotions, perhaps more so than ever before.

Remember, exploring food, the diversity of your own eating habits, and the acceptance of differences, is to explore and to realize different aspects of yourself.

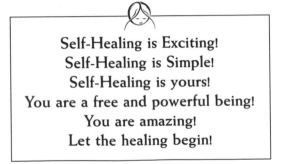

Self-Healing is Exciting!
Self-Healing is Simple!
Self-Healing is yours!
You are a free and powerful being!
You are amazing!
Let the healing begin!

Chapter 9

Simple Self-Healing Exercises

ༀ

The following exercises can be used individually, or in combinations both during and outside a healing session. Remember to always keep healing simple. Go with the flow, and do what you feel is right for you.

Getting ready

To get ready for the following self-healing, clearing and meditation exercises, please follow these basic instructions whenever possible, as they are conducive to positive results:

- Remove watch, jewelry, shoes or other footwear;
- Find a quiet peaceful, healing space inside or outside;
- Turn off all distractions such as television, radio, telephone, etc.;
- Wear loose fitting clothing if possible or at least undo waistbands, collar and buttons;
- Avoid eating a heavy meal immediately before the exercise;
- Tell yourself mentally that you are now ready to work

on the highest possible level, and that you are drawing easily to you all that you need;

- Decide how much time you want to spend on the exercise and take steps to make sure you remain undisturbed during that time;

Do not turn the exercises into a regime; do not push yourself to do them on days and at times that don't feel right or comfortable. Instead, it is much wiser to take that time for what you feel or wish to do.

1. Sitting down and being still

This first exercise allows you to step out of the everyday routines and patterns, to be still with yourself, and to experience your own sense of time. Begin by turning off the radio or television. Sit down comfortably. Do not cross your arms or legs. Keep your head straight. Relax your shoulders and the rest of your body. Breathe slowly from the bottom of your stomach with your mouth slightly open. Keep your eyes open for a while, then close them if you feel the need. Listen to your breathing. Allow yourself to feel connected to your body and to your breathing. Let thoughts come and go across your mind, not holding on to any one thought in particular.

Enjoy the stillness and silence around you. Enjoy the busyness of your mind. Stay in this position for ten minutes, doing nothing but breathing. You may find that your mind wants to get up and do something much sooner. Be firm and stay sitting. Over time, you will find this exercise relaxing and empowering. It's also a great way to reconnect with yourself.

2. Looking into the mirror

When I begin to work with clients over a period of time

to develop their own awareness and psychic abilities, I ask them to look at themselves in a mirror. This is also an exercise that I highly recommend for anyone who is using self-healing. Simply, we need to be able to look at ourselves. What better way than a mirror? Every household owns one, if not several. Taking a good look at yourself in a mirror will achieve at least two objectives: First, you will look at your reflection shining back at you from the mirror. We do not often take enough time to do just that. Second, depending on your mood and how you feel about yourself, you will notice aspects of yourself that you had not noticed before. Some people will notice first the positives: I have a cute nose, nice eyes; I like my hair. Some will notice what they see as negatives: my eyes are too small; my nose is not straight; my skin looks blotchy. Others will observe the reflection of themselves and make more general or sweeping assessments: I look tired; I look old; I look happy; I look great.

Before starting this exercise, get comfortable. Sitting is preferable. Have a mirror in front of you, and decide on the distance that the mirror should be from your face. First, look at your face in the mirror, allowing yourself to make observations. Then move on to looking at your face without making judgments. For example, if you judge your nose as too large or your smile as crooked, tell yourself now: "Enough!" Continue to look at your face and features and have the thought in your mind: "I love myself completely without condition." Say this clearly and firmly in your mind three or four times. At this point, you may feel that your chest, or heart center, opens and you may experience warmth in this area. Enjoy the moment.

Take a break now for a couple of minutes and allow your face to relax by opening your eyes wide twice. Open your mouth wide and stick out your tongue. Rub your forehead and the area just underneath your eyes, gently touching, massaging and loosening the skin and facial features. When you are ready, go ahead and look at your face again in the mirror. This time, look straight into your eyes. Try to remain looking into both eyes rather than selecting one. Do not look for anything in particular, but keep looking. If you feel strongly that you have to close your eyes, just close them and notice any interesting colors or pictures in your mind. Some of the possibilities that you may see as you are looking into your own eyes might include: your face disappearing for moments; your features fading and only an outline of your face and head being reflected back to you; you may notice a face looking back at you that looks familiar to you, but one that is not you as you see yourself everyday; you might see yourself as being very old, or a lot younger than you are presently. Another possibility is, if you are a man, to see a woman looking back at you, and vice versa. This can be both surprising and exhilarating the first time it happens. Just stay calm and deal with any fearful feeling you might have. The person staring back at you is not a stranger, a ghost or alien entity. The person staring back at you as you gaze into the mirror is you; it is a part of you. It can be someone you have already been, or someone for you to become. You may see it as a part of you that you are being at the same time as the "you now" that you know so well. It is important to be open to the acceptance of seeing and realizing those other parts of yourself you may see while looking at yourself. Remember that you are in control, and you will not see any part of you that you cannot handle.

Looking at yourself can be useful and beneficial. It can be classified under the headings of "letting go," "illumination," "realization" or "expansion of awareness." When you are using this exercise, it is important to remember not to expect to see anything of a specific nature, but rather to look and relax. Do not push to make things happen, as this can block your experience. The letting go that occurs during this exercise is one of a most positive healing nature. Enjoy some deep breathing with this exercise. When you feel that you are finished looking, close your eyes for a few minutes; let your body and mind relax. Surround yourself with yellow, blue, pink, purple, green, orange or white light if you feel the need. Initially, I would recommend ten to fifteen minute sessions. As you use this exercise more often, you can easily find yourself sitting for thirty to forty minutes as it becomes both fascinating and relaxing.

3. Opening the chakras or energy centers

This clearing meditation will be of invaluable help during your self-healing process. You can use it as a beginning basic focus until you find your own personal ways of clearing and healing yourself. This exercise can be used at any time of the day or night.

Before you begin this exercise you might want to take a relaxing shower or bath or stretch your body for a few minutes. This will help you to relieve tension, relax, loosen up and focus. It will also enable you to be present in the moment, and more in touch with your body. Dress in loose, comfortable clothes, no shoes, and no watches or jewelry. Feel comfortable. Do not eat a heavy meal at least an hour before you start this exercise. Turn off the radio, television, telephone and other distractions and allow yourself at least ten to thirty minutes without interruption. Then choose a quiet comfortable spot inside or outside of the house. Most people prefer to close their eyes during this exercise; however, there is no right or wrong, the choice is yours.

When you are ready to start, sit comfortably. Keep your head up straight. Do not cross or fold your feet, legs, or arms. I mention this because your body is like a circuit with a natural flow, and it is desirable to let the circuit flow naturally without crossing wires, so to speak, just like a battery. Now begin to breathe deeply from the bottom of your stomach. Let your thoughts come and go, allow any stress and tension to evaporate from your body. Be aware of your breathing and any sounds, feelings and smells around you. When you are ready, and feeling comfortable and relaxed, focus your mind on your stomach area. Imagine that this area is wide open and that there is nothing there at all, just a big, open, empty space. Take your time and relax.

Now begin to notice how your stomach feels. Does it feel like a particular color? Does any picture or symbol come to your mind? If not, ask yourself to feel what color it might be. Initially it may be a little unusual for you to think in color, but keep going, it will become easier. Remember to go with what you feel rather than what you think, and allow yourself to feel comfortable, open, and relaxed. If the stomach area, this particular space, feels heavy or blocked or nervous, just imagine that you are flooding it with your mind with a beautiful color or bright light until it feels calm and comfortable.

You can choose any color to use in this exercise. I suggest yellow, orange, white, gold or perhaps lavender or blue. If you do have a block in this place, just place one hand on the stomach for a few moments to help you relax, or gently rub and massage the area. A block might feel like a heavy or a dark area, or simply something that is in the way of you flowing and moving.

When you are ready, continue to relax and feel at one with your breathing. Do this for a few moments, breathing in and breathing out, just imagining the air, the breath, going all through your body. Imagine that each time you breathe in, you are breathing in everything new and each time you breathe out, you are letting go of everything you don't need. Have the thought once in your mind: "I am letting go of everything I no longer need."

Now you are ready to move on to the chest area. Imagine your chest is also wide open and that there is nothing there at all, just a big, open, empty space, just as you did with the stomach. When you first work with the chest area, also known as the heart center, you may feel flooded with an emotional, warm, loving feeling. It can be a powerful, wonderful feeling. So enjoy the sensations and ask yourself: "How does this place feel? What color is it?" Do any images come to your mind? Again, if the color is one you like and feel comfortable with in this place, then that's great. If it's a color that you don't like or don't feel good with, change it with your mind to one that you feel good about. Persist with making the change. You can do this. Remember, change any heaviness or weight in this area by flooding it with bright light or color using your mind and imagining this happening. It will, so do not give up. If you have a problem with this, examine anything inside of you that tells you that you cannot do this. But do not allow it to stop you making change because your mind, when focused, is stronger than any obstacle or objection.

If you have any problem with real heaviness or pain in either the stomach or the chest, it may help to just place your hands flat on these areas and allow them to be calmed and soothed. You could also rub very gently in slow, circular movements. Give yourself time to do this. There is no rush. It's all right. And if you don't see or feel colors immediately or much of anything else going on, it's all right too. It doesn't matter. Don't push or feel you cannot do this, because you will begin to be more in touch with these places after a few sessions.

There is also a space between the heart center and stomach, around the rib cage base, where you may feel deep emotional pain, fear, anger. You may recognize that this area is blocked. If you do feel a weight or tightness in these areas, as well as in the stomach and the heart center, you may use lavender oil or rose oil once a day for a week to ten days. Just place a few drops of the oil on the area you want to work with and then massage it around in slow, circular movements. Dilute the oil if you have sensitive skin. These two places—the chest and stomach—are emotion centers, so this is why they often feel heavy or blocked; they are storing emotional pain.

Interestingly, psychology is just starting to call the stomach "the little brain" and realizing its importance. Other places in our body are also being recognized as areas that store rage, frustration and suppression. John Sarno, MD, thinks that virtually all lower back pains are caused not by structural abnormalities but by repressed rage. He has written three books on the subject, the latest being *The Mind Body Prescription* (Warner Books, 1998). I have always recognized lower back pain as a sure sign of a build-up of anger and frustration that the person is hanging on to. It almost always is. If you have been living for a long time with the feeling of a heavy weight on your chest or stomach, physical pain or even shortness of breath, you may need a rebirthing session or another similar process to release these emotions.

When you are ready to continue the exercise, move on to the throat. Repeat the process you have used for the stomach and chest, noticing and being aware of how this space is clearing, how blocks are being removed, and how you are bringing color, light and balance wherever you feel the need. The throat is an interesting reference point as it can be seen as the communication center, which often becomes blocked when we are holding back from expressing ourselves. At times, we literally feel as if something is stuck in our throat. Have you noticed how many people seem to have a nervous cough, often living with the affliction for years without wondering why it is there and what it is really about?

Next, move on to your forehead. Imagine a wide, open, empty space. Go through the process as with the other points, noticing any colors or images or blocks. Then to complete the process move on to the very top of your head. Imagine that the very top of your head is also wide open, nothing there at all, just a big, empty space.

When you have gone through these centers—the stomach, the chest, the throat, the forehead, and the top of your head—fill each of these centers with a beautiful color of your choice or a bright light. Imagine that every single one is filling up with bright light, color and energy. Now allow yourself to relax and bathe and breathe the color, light and energy all through your body, as well as these centers. Enjoy the sensations. When you have finished, if you feel that you would like to leave these centers open, you may do so. If you feel the need to close them, then just go back through each one and mentally close them. To do this is quite simple. Just as you imagined each one opening, imagine that each one is closing and shutting like a door.

After this exercise you will feel good, even great. If you feel a little bit vulnerable or still open and don't feel comfortable with that, just imagine that you are being completely surrounded by a beautiful gold light that reaches over the top of your head and goes right underneath your feet. The shape of this light could be a bubble or a circle or a pyramid or a cloud, whatever feels right to you.

This cleansing, releasing and healing of the centers exercise is an invaluable basis for self-healing. It can be used once or twice a week or as often as you wish to check how you feel and what shape your body is in, and to clear and heal when needed. Remember, if you follow the threads of your feelings and awareness, each center will lead you to other areas of your body. Then you can check the whole "you" rather than just parts.

4. Ears

Earlier I mentioned the ears as one of my own chosen

reference points or chakras. The ears play a great role in our body, that of balance. The following exercise can be used to clear any blockage in the ear, to relieve any pain in the ears, to bring balance to either or both sides of the body, and to improve and enhance hearing capacity and capabilities.

Get ready and sit comfortably. Take a few minutes to breathe and calm yourself. When you feel ready, imagine that your ears are wide open from the inside. Now imagine them expanding from the inside, imagine they are getting bigger and bigger. Now listen to everything that you hear: a dog barking outside, a faint humming in the background, a telephone ringing in another room. Be aware of all sounds. When you have done this and recognized outside sounds (by "outside," I mean "outside of yourself") flood both of your ears with light by imagining a beautiful bright white, gold, yellow or blue light.

You can go on to improve your hearing by continuing this exercise, by imagining that, like a radio, you are now going to change channels and that your ears are open to other wavelengths. Take your time and notice any other new or different sounds. In the beginning, you might not physically hear other sounds, but they may come to your mind as a thought. For instance, a bell ringing, perhaps people talking, and the sound of the sea or wind. Just accept these thoughts and sounds, or whatever you hear or feel, for at least five minutes. If you hear something but cannot pinpoint exactly what it is, imagine that, as with a radio, you are in control and that you are now going to turn up the volume of your own hearing until you hear clearly and recognize what you hear. If repeated regularly—I suggest once or twice a week—this exercise will develop your awareness of the delicate balance within your inner ears and improve your hearing. It will be a major start to developing clairaudience, which means clear hearing, so that you can begin to hear on other wavelengths besides the obvious everyday ones. This exercise is also great for cleaning any blocks you might have regarding listening to yourself and others.

5. Opening your senses

Remove your watch, jewelry, shoes, etc. Sit down in a comfortable and relaxed position. Do not cross your arms or legs. Keep your head up. With eyes open or closed, start to breathe through your mouth deeply from your stomach. Take a few minutes to do this. When you are ready, you can begin to visualize opening your ears and noticing all the sounds in and around you. Next, use your sense of smell and concentrate on anything that you smell, distinguishing each and every separate aroma. Now, open your mouth wide, stick out your tongue and just leave it there for a few moments. No need to feel ridiculous. You are alone. How does it feel? What do you taste in the air? Take your time. When you are ready, put your tongue back in your mouth.

Now take a few slow deep breaths and imagine that every single pore of skin on your body is completely wide open. How does that feel? It might feel like a whoosh of energy, a great lightness. You may even become so sensitive that you can almost feel a very small insect or even a particle of dust as it lands on your skin. For a few minutes enjoy the freedom of this exercise. When you have finished, if you wish to close down all the pores of your skin, go ahead by simply visualizing them closing. You can also use the thought "I am drawing easily to myself all that I need", before finishing this exercise.

6. Exploring your hands

Hands and feet are great energy points to massage and work with, as they connect all areas of the body and contain many nerve endings. So check them both regularly. By checking, I mean gently massage them with the use of oil or lotion, and feel each part of the feet and back of the hands. If you feel any hard lumps or tender places, apply slight pressure to these areas, hold that pressure for a few moments, then release and repeat. In time, you will become skilled in this practice. Remember, so much can be released with these simple steps.

You could also buy a book or a set of cards that show the basic pressure points corresponding to the different organs in various parts of the body. This is called reflexology. I suggest obtaining a wallet- size plastic card from the Institute of Reflexology (PO Box 12642 St. Petersburg, FL 33733 USA). The inexpensive card shows on one side the feet with pressure points and corresponding vital organs and body organs, and on the other side the hands with the same information. Have fun working with these cards or books. But remember, even though it is written that a certain point corresponds to a certain part of your body, you may find as you are touching or adding pressure to a certain point in your hands and feet that a totally different area of your body is affected. So experiment with yourself, and accept your own findings as well as what is written. A trip to a reflexologist at least once could also be beneficial so that you can watch how a specialist works with your hands and feet. Ask questions during your visit so that you gain a greater understanding and pick up tips on different techniques. This will also help you find out how your body acts and reacts during the release process when you work alone. You could also, quite simply, trust yourself, without the use of cards, books or specialists.

Start your own session by getting in a relaxed state. Take a few moments to stretch out your body, further releasing any built-up tension. When you are ready, sit comfortably, not crossing your arms or legs, and take some oil, body lotion or hand cream. Start with your hands. Work the liquid into the front and back of the hands, then continue by working the liquid into each finger, front and back. Now rub your hands together, exerting some pressure so that you can really feel them and feel that you are connected to both of them. Now, with whichever hand you write with, use your thumb to massage all over the opposite hand with gentle pressure. Notice if you feel any lumps, knots, hard places or any areas that feel tender to the touch. Look for these on the palm, the front of the hand, the back of the hand, and both sides of the fingers. If you find any such places, work on them by adding pressure with your thumb and hold that pressure for a few moments, then release after perhaps five or ten seconds. Repeat this process once or twice, and then continue to massage that area with slow circular movements. While you are doing this be aware of how your body and your head feels. Do you feel any pain or release going on anywhere else besides your hands? Take your time and you will be surprised at how quickly you develop your own sense of which points of your hands and feet are connected to various body parts and organs. Develop trust in your own abilities to know what to do in the moment. This is important, so believe what you feel.

Take your time working with this hand and massage your wrist when you have finished. Take a few moments to relax, and then, when you are ready, repeat the process with the other hand.

It is very possible that you might find connections right away with parts of your hands corresponding to other body parts and organs, or it may take a few sessions before you feel anything. But keep working on this; you will benefit. When you have finished working on both hands rub them together and then pretend that you are washing your hands, making those movements. Just by rubbing your hands together and making this washing movement, you are clearing, stimulating and revitalizing many energy points and centers throughout your body.

7. Footbath

When working on the feet, follow the same procedures you used when working with the hands. The footbath I describe here is something I picked up in India some years ago. I have heard explanations that salt draws out and negates blocked energies. I am not sure that this is so, but salt definitely has proved to be a plus in this exercise. Hot water, salt and oils without doubt help not only the feet to relax but also the whole body. This calming effect is a perfect way to clear stress and to open into a positive healing ambience and space. This footbath can be a healing work session by itself, or it can be combined with opening and cleaning the energy centers, either the ones you have chosen or the following ones: stomach, chest, throat, forehead and top of the head.

Start by soaking your feet in a bowl or tub of comfortably hot water with a few drops of your favorite oil. I highly recommend Lavender, Rose or Sandalwood. Also add three to four large handfuls of sea salt, which can be easily found in most large grocery stores.

If you wish to open and clean your energy centers, place both feet flat in the bucket. Sit comfortably with your head up and your hands, palms upwards, lying flat on your knees or lap. Breathe deeply from the bottom of your stomach. Enjoy the aroma from the hot water and take a few moments to relax, concentrating only on your breathing. You may keep your eyes open or closed during this session. Keeping them closed will work best if you have a lot of visual stimulus around you that may distract your attention. When you feel ready, go through all of the chakras or energy centers. Notice how each one looks and feels. Clear any blocks or heavy feeling by flooding each one with a color and light of your choice, as we have done in the chakra exercise. Keep your head up straight, and keep breathing. When you have finished, visualize your whole body being flooded with bright color and light of your choice. When you are done, simply enjoy the moment of feeling calm, open, peaceful, relaxed and energized. Remove your feet from the water when it is cooled, dry them and take a few more moments to enjoy your positive feeling.

If you do not wish to include opening and cleaning the energy centers, soak your feet for five to ten minutes or until the water becomes cool and then gently towel dry both feet.

Now massage your feet and work with them in the same ways that you did with your hands using oil or lotion. Work with the tops of your feet, the bottoms, the sides, and also the toes, one by one. Remember also to massage the ankles. As with the hands, look for lumps, bumps and tender places and apply pressure release. Then massage your feet as you did with the hands. Use your creativity when working with your hands and feet. You may use kneading motions, gentle pulling or stretching, or bending movements, whatever feels good and right for you.

Working with your hands and feet in this way is not only a great way to relax, to feel good, to connect with your body, to clear energy and release toxins throughout your body, but it is also a great way for you to make connections to and pinpoint those parts of your body that need healing. Never underestimate the importance and value of simple techniques.

8. Headache

The next time you find yourself with a headache, take time to practice your healing techniques and abilities by clearing it yourself. Make a point of not reaching for the aspirin or painkiller as an immediate answer. Sit still and breathe deeply from your stomach. Tell yourself: "I am letting go of everything I no longer need." Place both hands on your head; add pressure to the various pressure points you will find around your head, neck and shoulders. Try this for a few seconds and then release. Then try again. See what works. Use this technique also in other parts of your body when needed. Keep practicing and working on particular points and areas that are giving you problems. Keep exploring and discovering. Remember, **you** are the healer; you just need to discover how **you** work.

If you do have a blinding headache, one of the first things to do is to breathe deeply and imagine that the top of your head is wide open and that tension is leaving. Other things that might work are breathing deeply, fresh air, drinking water, eating something light without a lot of sugar, taking a bath, or a walk. Work on it. See what works for you. Keep going. This is something you can also do for a family member or a friend. Experiment and do what feels right for you to do at the moment even if it seems strange or does not appear to make sense. If you feel a little foolish doing this with a friend, don't allow that feeling to stop you. Tell yourself to keep going and just wait and see what happens. Practice really does make perfect. So give yourself a chance. Become aware by being observant. What generally gives you a headache? Notice any particular patterns. Ask yourself, "What do I need?" Notice if there was any one thing that you did which cleared the headache, or whether it was a combination of things that brought relief and the end of the headache.

9. The throat

If you feel you have something stuck in your throat or a nervous cough, you need to look at communication. How long has this problem been there? You could be holding back your self-expression, not saying what you really want to say.

So go ahead. Say it. Or at least recognize that you want to speak. What is it that you want to say and to whom? Write it down. If you feel you cannot verbalize what you want and need to say, the important thing to do is to get release. Throat problems and communication problems can often be resolved quickly by these simple actions alone. However you can go further by visualizing a band of yellow, gold or orange around your neck and mentally resolve that this color will stay there and continue to heal and soothe even when you have stopped thinking of it. You might also take a yellow, gold or orange scarf and wear it around your throat and neck for the day. If you feel a sore or dry throat coming on, decide to deal with it before it gets worse. Know that it does not have to get worse and reach a climax; you can decide not to have a sore throat. After you have taken action, take a moment to find out what your throat is telling you. What is it really saying to you? And then deal with the physical manifestation in any of the above ways, or simply tell yourself that this is now the end of the imbalance. Mean it and believe it, with no room whatsoever for doubt.

10. Nervous Stomach

Stomach or other digestive system problems, anxiety related or not, are very common; we all experience them at some point in our lives. Problems can range from physical pain to a heavy bloated feeling through to medically diagnosed problems such as ulcers, irritable bowel syndrome, colon cancer, gastroenteritis, and colic to name just a few. Whatever problems you are having related to the stomach, be it as simple as a nervous stomach or diarrhea or something much more serious, you will obtain remarkable results using the following exercise. As always, take time to ask yourself: Why do I have a stomach problem? What is my body telling me? Where does this current situation come from?

Then, when you are ready, start by lying on your stomach on the floor and allow that part of you to completely relax. Just feel the tension flowing away. Have the thought in mind: "I am letting go of everything I no longer need." Stay in this position for ten minutes. Or try turning on your back and placing your hands on the stomach and massaging with slow, circular motions, perhaps using plain oil or even peppermint oil. This simple action could be your answer. Stomach problems are usually quite easy to deal with if you commit yourself to action, right through a simple nervous stomach to serious conditions. Keep working on it. You will see results.

11. Sexual Energy

The genital area is a recognized chakra or energy center. Sexual energy can be a very powerful force which you can move around your body at will. Suppression of sexual energy can lead to imbalance. It is generally accepted that this energy center is located between the base of your spine and your navel, in the lower abdomen area. Many people may feel and recognize it to be below the navel in the sexual parts of their body. When they locate this area, they often feel warmth.

The next time you have a deep sexual orgasm, relax completely. Feel the energy in your genital area and allow it to flow and move as if feeding and flooding your entire body. Be aware of this energy flow and let it happen without being too detailed on where the energy is directed. You might want to read a book on Tantra practices, which use techniques that control sexual energy, taking it all through the chakra points and then releasing it through the top of the head. Some of you might have had an experience of a powerful headache just before or after sexual orgasm. This is a build-up of sexual energy going straight to the top of the head through the body without finding a release. If you experience a headache or tension during sex, that is a good time to visualize the top of your head being open for release. You could also use your mind and your feelings to sense and redirect the flow of energy to other energy centers or other body parts. I notice that a lot of people, especially women, when they do not have a release of this energy, often store sexual energy in the lower back area of the base of the spine. It can often cause problems such as a lower back pain, which has no apparent medical cause yet is very real to the sufferer.

12. Letting go

This exercise can be used to deal with insomnia and other problems relating to the nervous system, thyroid problems, eating disorders, skin conditions, lupus, rheumatism and arthritis. You can use it for just about anything that requires the body to let go of emotions such as pain, fear, trauma, anxiety and stress.

Begin by removing your watch, any jewelry and your shoes. Lie down flat on your stomach on the floor or another comfortable surface. Use a pillow or a cushion for your head if you need one. Now let go everything for a few minutes, take deep relaxing breaths from the bottom of your stomach and allow your whole body to relax. Allow your thoughts to come and go. Do not try to clear your mind. After ten minutes or so, have this one thought clearly in your mind twice: "I am letting go of everything I no longer need." Now continue to breathe and relax. Allow your body to completely let go and feel as if you are sinking into and becoming one with the flat surface.

Imagine now that you are flowing and moving like a river, that every tension and stress is being released from your body, rolling and falling away. When you have finished, just continue to be still and enjoy the calm, peaceful feeling. Take your time, and when you are done, get up slowly. Before finishing, you might imagine a beautiful color, one of your own choice, surrounding, bathing, and enveloping you, feeding and energizing your whole body and being. Take long, slow deep breaths and breathe this color all through your body. I like to use orange, yellow, purple or white.

After a few days or a week using this exercise, you will be amazed at how much more relaxed, stress-free, and in control you feel. I recommend this exercise to be done lying on your stomach because this is the area where we hold much of our emotions. If this does feel very difficult or uncomfortable for you, you can lie on your back and you will still benefit greatly from the exercise.

13. Letting go using focus points

Choose the most peaceful setting for this exercise—a quiet room, a beautiful or open outside space, or wherever you feel comfortable. Get ready by removing your watch, jewelry, shoes and any tight belts. Undo the top buttons of shirts and loosen waistbands. Loosen up your body by stretching it out for a couple of minutes. Turn off the radio and television. I like to do this exercise sitting in a simple straight-backed chair. You might feel like sitting on the floor. Go with whatever feels good for you. Do not cross your arms, legs or feet.

Now find something to look at. I use a small, multi-faceted Austrian crystal ball or pendent available at most jewelry stores, the type you can hang in your window. You can also use an incense stick as a focus by looking at the glowing lighted end, or a burning candle flame, or perhaps just a simple item in your everyday surroundings that captures your attention. Whatever you decide to focus on, keep your eyes fixed on that point. Let your body relax and take a few deep breaths. Keep your eyes gazing at that particular point on which you are focusing. Breathe deeply from the bottom of your stomach through your mouth and take a few minutes to listen to and enjoy yourself breathing in and out. Take time to observe any sounds around you. Remain still and calm, letting your thoughts come and go. Now stay like this for ten minutes and when you feel that it is enough, take your time and slowly get up. (If you find it difficult to be still for ten minutes, then taking a hot relaxing bath first may help.) You can add to this exercise by visualizing yourself being surrounded by beautiful lilac or blue light and then breathing the color all through your body.

While you are gazing and focusing on your specific object, if at any point you really feel like closing your eyes, just go ahead and do so. Continue to be aware of your breathing and of outside noise. As you allow yourself to become absorbed by the quietness and calmness of this exercise, you may feel a surprising amount of your own inner strength and a feeling of centeredness. However, if it is really impossible for you to be still for ten minutes, a rebirthing may be necessary. Many people who are carrying intense emotions find it hard to slow down and be still. So it could be that you have a deeper core issue to explore. Do be patient with yourself.

14. Letting go and cleaning

There is another way to let go, which I highly recommend. I would like to share with you the story of how it came into being for me. I had unconsciously used this technique for many years but it came into my conscious awareness after a telephone conversation with two people who I cared about very much. They were both angry at each other. Both were telling me their different sides of the story, and of all the months' previous events which had led them to their mutual anger and their impasse in communication.

Long after the telephone call, their situation was still on my mind. For about twenty minutes, I recounted the whole telephone conversation to my husband. He listened patiently, adding a few comments of his own, which I made a note of. For me, this first stage was a laying out of the situation that I was consumed with and the first step towards letting it go. Next, I sat at my computer and made notes of what I would say step-by-step in the next telephone conversation with these two people. I wanted to put things in perspective for them and point out other options they had to resolve the conflict. I read my typed piece through once. Then I clearly numbered each point that I had made. I felt satisfied because I had taken action. I pushed my chair back from the keyboard and stood up.

In doing this, I felt a couple of great things happen. First, as I stood up, I felt a huge weight drop from my chest and watched it falling to the ground. It was a mass of non-physical matter. Then my attention was drawn to the top of my head, which I realized was behaving and looking like a fountain. It was beautiful. Every color of the rainbow was cascading from the top of my head to the floor. There appeared to be an open hole at the top of my head. I could also see and feel at the top of my head something that looked like a Centurion's helmet. It was built from solid-looking layers of different colors. Then I let my fingers run across my forehead through my hair to the back of my head. I watched, delighted, as a block of non-physical matter, which felt solid all across my forehead, was actually moved backwards and then started to run and flow with the fountain off my head and body to the ground. I repeated the movement with my hand. The process happened again and again.

Meanwhile I began to feel more and more relaxed and energized. The block was almost cleared. Next I went outside. I stood up straight with my feet apart, parallel to each other. I took a few deep breaths and fixed both of my eyes on a far point straight ahead of me. I continued slowly the movement with my hand, running it from my forehead to the back of my head. I did this a few times. I saw and felt that the left side of my head was also blocked, and felt and watched that block shift. Next I noticed a block in my left hip area and also at the bottom of my stomach. Then I found myself somewhere else in my body. I could not tell where exactly, but it was amazing because I saw two large channels, which looked like big pipes. They were also cleaning themselves. I was aware that these two channels had not been cleaned for perhaps hundreds of years since I had last been in touch with them. I was glad for this realization and continued with the process. After ten minutes, I felt wonderful—perfectly clear and perfectly calm.

The following is a very simple healing, balancing, clearing and energizing exercise based on this experience. Have fun with it and discover new ways and additions for yourself.

Stand up straight, head held up. Position your feet apart and parallel. Fix your eyes on a point straight ahead of you and try to sense a line running down your forehead, chin, throat, chest and stomach. Imagine this line is going right through your navel. The imaginary line will bring both balance and focus so that the two separate halves of you, both right and left, can clear and align themselves. You can also use a tree in this way. In this case, put one foot each side of the tree and place your body, forehead, chest, and stomach gently on the tree. Keep your head upright. Now let go.

Letting go happens in two ways. Let the top of your head be open to connect with the "all that is" in the universe. Let also anything and everything you don't need fall to the ground through your feet. You can also boost your own energy by tracing the roots of the tree with your mind. You can see the roots under the ground or your emotions may feel the roots spreading out in all directions. Now allow yourself to draw back into yourself, from the four corners of the earth and beyond where these roots reach, all of the energy and clarity that you need at this time.

15. Expanding and contracting

This exercise allows you to draw into yourself what you need and release what you no longer want. It also incorporates deep breathing and visualization techniques. It can be of enormous benefit when you feel as if life has stopped or that you are in a corner and no longer have much control. This exercise allows you to experience the "all that is" and make use of it. It allows your illness, disease and imbalances to become impersonal, which can be a useful tool in the healing process.

Sit comfortably and prepare yourself as with previous exercises. It is advisable not to do this exercise after eating a heavy meal as you may find it hard to concentrate or even drift off to sleep. Begin by taking long, slow deep breaths from the bottom of your stomach, through your mouth. Relax and make sure that you are not holding any tension anywhere in your body. Let your thoughts come and go, but do not try to clear your mind. There is no need to try to clear your mind because, at some point, it will clear itself. One day you may become aware that your mind is empty, that you are not thinking about anything at all. After a while, choose a point or energy center of your body. Easy ones include the stomach, chest or forehead. Imagine that you are centered in and are coming from that particular place. Take your time. Now imagine you are getting bigger and bigger in that place. Soon you are expanding from this place and your essence is filling the room. You can stay in the room filling that space or you can expand more and more, filling the street, the town, the country, and the world going onward and outward and exploring the universe. It is your choice how far you expand. Take a few minutes to enjoy that expanded feeling. While you are in the expanded state, have this thought in your mind just once: "I am drawing easily to myself all that I need." When you are ready, come back. Contract inwards, back to the point in your body where you started. You can come back very slowly, very fast, or anything in between. Play with this and enjoy the sensations. You will find after a while that you are in control of this coming and going, with very little thought or effort.

Now be still. You are completely back in your body and centered in your body. Be aware of your own breathing once again. You may add to this exercise the visualization routine of being surrounded by color and light. You can also end with the positive affirmation: "I am of pure light and pure energy." Enjoy afterwards your empowered and relaxed state, and breathe it all through your body until you feel full.

16. Body combing

Use the following exercise for a general clearing of your own personal space and to immediately change your mood and perception. You do not necessarily have to get ready for this exercise, although removing your watch is a good idea.

Sitting or standing, begin by laying the palm of your hand flat about four inches above the top of your head, then move to the neck, then the shoulders and right down to your waist. Imagine any build-up that you do not need falling to the floor. Keep combing your body, back and front. If your arm gets tired, change to the other one. When you have finished the top half of your body, do the same for the bottom half. Then, using both hands, imagine that you are brushing down new energies all over and through your body. If you have aches and pains, or problem areas, work on these for a few minutes by brushing and sweeping these areas with your open hand. Do not touch the body with your hands, but stay about four inches from it. Next, kick out your feet and legs for a few minutes, stretch both arms out wide to your sides, so that you look like a bird in flight, and let your arms flap up and down as if you were flying. Now let your arms relax, hanging by your sides. Turn from your waist slowly to one side, then to the other. Now, stretch your back. Finally, touch your face and forehead with your hands and gently rub, lift and massage the skin.

You can add anything you feel to do to this exercise. Just remember that it is a sweeping, clearing exercise to bring positive change. When you are done, you will feel significantly different in a bright and positive way. Remember that healing your body also means healing your own space around your physical body.

17. Balance and focus

This exercise can be used before you begin a self-healing session and can also be used regularly to stay in balance and focused on both a mind and body level. I recommend doing this exercise first thing in the morning or at the start of your day if you work at night. However, this exercise is not limited to beginnings of time periods; it can and should be used whenever you feel the need for balance and focus—the need to get back to yourself and see where you stand at any given moment.

First, stand straight. Keep both feet apart pointing parallel. Keep your head up straight. Relax your shoulders. Now, with one finger, draw a line from your forehead down your nose, down through your throat, your chest, your stomach, right through to the base of your body. Feel this line. Imagine this line. Imagine that it is your centerline and that you are going to arrange your body so that exactly half of your body is each side of the line.

To balance yourself, rotate your shoulders backwards and forwards and up and down for a few moments. Kick out your feet. Get comfortable. Get your feet parallel again. Now bend your knees slightly to redistribute your weight until it feels absolutely comfortable and perfect. Keep your head up straight. Once again, draw the thin line down your forehead, nose, and through your body. Do whatever it takes to feel the balance, shifting your body weight slightly to the left or right as needed.

When you feel that you are balanced on both sides of the line, and your body is equally distributed, take a moment to imagine that your feet are like the roots of a strong tree and that the thin line reaches through your body and continues out of the top of your head and is connected to the universe and the "all that is." Feel now that you are in balance and a part of the "all that is." Feel how wonderful and powerful this feels. Enjoy the feeling and the moment.

Keep your head up straight and take a few long, slow, deep breaths from your stomach. If you wish, you can now mentally let go through all of your energy centers, opening them and letting go everything you don't need. At this point, you might like to use the positive affirmation: "I am of pure light and pure energy." Just feel yourself being that and drawing to yourself everything you need.

When you have finished the exercise, if you wish, you can visualize yourself standing in a pyramid of light and color, or a bubble, or just being surrounded by light and color. Remember to have your chosen color and light form go over the top of your head and also under the bottom of your feet.

Whenever you feel dull-headed, or blocked, or out of focus, rub your forehead backwards and forwards for a few minutes. Massage the back of your neck. And then go into this balancing and focusing routine. You can keep your eyes open or closed during this exercise. I suggest keeping your gaze fixed on a distant point. Enjoy the balance from the session and decide to make balance a part of your life. This exercise can be used first thing in the morning to start your day on a positive, balanced and focused track, or at any point during the day when you feel the need to become centered, solid, and back in touch with yourself. It works also to bring you consciously into an awareness of you, the present moment and state of your being.

Chapter 10

True Stories

⸙

Introduction

Welcome to some true stories of people who have used self-healing to change their lives. My wish is that these stories will delight, entertain and inspire you. These people are not extraordinary; they are people just like you and I. They have in common the desire to be well and the desire for change. They each saw and proved to themselves, and to us all, that self-healing is possible.

Although some of these people initially came to visit me, and I may have even been, for some, instrumental in their healing process, there are millions of other people that I have not met who are discovering and using self-healing in their lives every day.

Complete self-belief

I met Josh, an eight-year-old boy, a couple of years ago. His mother brought him because she was concerned about his eyes. Josh had to wear glasses and he hated them. He had three different kinds and didn't like any of them. Josh had been diagnosed with esotropia, an overactive inferior oblique eye problem, also known as crossed eyes, that would make one eye turn inward. He had had surgery on both eyes to loosen the eye muscles and make them both even. However, the doctor overcompensated and left a muscle too loose, thus the eye began to turn to the outside. His mother did not want Josh to have further surgery, although it had been strongly recommended.

I had several sessions with Josh, getting to know him, seeing how his eyes were working, and giving healing. I recommended that his mother get a copy of the Bates Eye Method and use the exercises with Josh for a short while. He followed them for a couple of weeks, exercising first one eye and then the other. I also explained to Josh how he could help heal himself. I told him to visualize every day a beautiful white or yellow light bathing, soothing and making his eyes well, and to touch them with his hands. I let him know that he needed to be in charge and make sure that both of his eyes did exactly what he told them to do, and that they worked well. Josh developed his own technique and used it on his eyes. His mother explained to me in an e-mail how Josh was healing himself:

"He knows when the 'bad' eye is moving involuntarily outwards. When it does, he simply closes both eyes, then, leaving the 'good' eye shut, opens only the 'bad' eye. He mentally tells himself that this eye is being lazy and that it has to work by itself now. Then, he talks to the eye, sometimes out loud and sometimes mentally. He tells it things like: 'You are just being a lazy eye and I am going to make you work hard too' or 'It's not fair to make the good eye do all the work, so you have to do it by yourself for a while'. If it is really bad during the day, he lays down on the sofa, or on the floor at school, and closes his eyes. He takes the palm of his hands and gently places them over his closed eyelids. Then moving his hands ever so slowly, he drags his fingers down across his eyes and face and continues this for about four minutes. He has his eye closed the entire time. He imagines that there is a bright yellow healing light on the tips of his fingers and he is dragging this bright, yellow light across his eyes. He also uses this last exercise every single night before going to sleep. He starts on his back in bed, takes deep breaths from his stomach about five times, and then tells himself that he is floating in the sky on a big white fluffy cloud. He can feel the cloud he is laying on beneath his feet, legs, back, shoulders and head. When he is totally 'floating', he proceeds with the yellow light touching his eyes as mentioned above."

Three months later, Josh's mother came back to visit. She was very pleased. Josh no longer needed to wear glasses. He was still doing his own self-healing, and his eyes were perfectly straight and working fine.

This little boy did most of the healing himself. I just got him started by showing him how. He believed he could heal and made healing a part of his everyday life. This illustrates quite well how self-healing works. It shows that thought is a powerful medium, and that the less fixed are our concepts, the less we block the process of self-healing.

Attention through illness and pain

Audrey was well into her seventies when she first came to see me. She was in great physical shape. She still drove her own car and was quite active. She was of Jewish-Italian descent and a grandmother from a somewhat matriarchal society. She was always very much in control, rarely letting down her guard. But when she relaxed, her face would break into a smile and it was as if a light had been turned on. At those times, she would look very young. Peter, her only son, had two grown daughters of his own, Audrey's beloved grandchildren. Peter had recently undergone major heart surgery and was recovering relatively well. Everything looked good for him, despite the fact that his wife of many years had been unable to cope emotionally while he was ill, and had left him. He was nearly finished going through a messy divorce and felt a real sense of abandonment. Audrey worried about the soon to be ex-daughter-in-law; she felt that this woman was unbalanced, and was not treating her son fairly on a financial level.

Audrey worried most of the time about all of the people around her. She worried about her family, her friends and her extended family, but nobody more than her son and his daughters. Audrey herself was a widow living alone. Her late husband had left a substantial amount of capital in the bank, and she wanted to make sure that when she died, the money would be given to her nearest and dearest, and that everyone would benefit and be taken care of. There were problems, however, with various cousins and she did not know which way to turn to keep everyone happy.

Audrey ate well, did not drink or smoke, and did not overindulge in anything. She came to see me because she had been in a lot of pain for some time, on and off, with her right hip. She had seen doctors and various specialists, and had had the area x-rayed many times, but nothing had shown up as the cause of her hip problem. Audrey had also tried alternatives such as acupuncture, various herbal remedies, and Polar therapy. Nothing had helped so far.

During our first session, as an intuitive, I was able to put her financial situation into perspective, giving her some solid answers about what would happen in the future. Afterwards, she felt a lot calmer and more satisfied and secure about the future, although she remained cautious. We continued to talk and slowly she became more visibly relaxed.

Audrey left that initial healing session feeling good and pain-free. I suspected, however, that her right hip was a sign of her sense of responsibility, and that she was keeping the pain there as a reminder to herself that suffering was necessary and that she wasn't going to leave this Earth until she had sorted everything out for everyone else in her life. In each subsequent session, it was evident that Audrey felt very grateful for what she had, but seemed to accept the belief that life could not be perfect or pain free. But she needed to pass on from this life being sure everything would be in order and taken care of according to her wishes.

Audrey had about four other healing sessions. Each time, the end result was the same. She would leave the session pain-free and would stay pain-free for a few days and sometimes a whole week. Then the pain would return, especially when she started to worry and become anxious.

I realized that Audrey had no one in her life to touch her on a daily basis. Yet she needed to be touched. She had no one to make her feel that she was the center of the universe and to give her undivided attention. But she had this deep need. In her youth Audrey had been a very sensual woman. But during the last five years of her marriage, her husband's serious illness meant that she had lived without an intimate physical relationship. She had not been touched or nurtured for a long time. Her hip problem was a cry for help, her way to remind herself of her own physical nurturing needs. Her pain was telling her to make at least some effort to see that her own needs were fulfilled. This was a major reason why Audrey came for healing sessions. The sessions were also a respite and a relief from the responsibility of all that she was going through, and everything that was happening around her, at that point in her life.

Once we sat down and talked about her personal needs, Audrey understood the situation. She could see clearly then that she was holding on to the hip problem and the pain. Later, she told me that she could live with the pain now that she knew why it was there. She stopped coming for healing. Letting go of her pain and moving on wasn't really an option for Audrey at that point. She said that, although it sounded strange, she almost needed the pain to be there.

Many months later, I saw Audrey at a local event. She

had found a good attorney and felt satisfied and relieved regarding her financial affairs. Everything was in order now and her son was well. Her hip was better, she said, and never hurt. She agreed that as her life had changed, so did the hip pain. She no longer needed it in her life. She told me that she was also going regularly for a massage and taking care of her need to be touched and nurtured. Audrey had finally decided to move on, and to take care of her own needs.

Self-punishment and guilt

Angela was a 24-year-old college student trying hard to improve herself in life. Some people would have judged her as promiscuous, but the fact is that she really enjoyed the intimacy and the attention that an active sex life brought her. She also had a lot of guilt about her sexual drive and activities with varied partners. She came to visit me completely devastated and very ashamed. She was feeling suicidal. She had contacted herpes and wanted to know which one of her lovers has transmitted the virus to her.

At first the situation seemed unbearable. Angela felt that the only way out was to take her own life. She was a religious person and felt she was being punished for her sexual activities. She felt condemned and unclean.

We started to look at why Angela had herpes. Why did she bring and allow that reality into her life? It came out that Angela had been sexually abused as a child and was still punishing herself. She believed that the abuse must have been her fault in some way.

This is very common among abuse victims, especially with those who have been abused as children. Could this self-blame come from the fact that children often do not feel enough self-worth and belief in themselves as children? Perhaps they feel that because they are very small and adults are so big and powerful, the adults must be right? This makes sense when we remember that, as children, we are often told what to eat, what we can and cannot do, and when to sleep. Although perhaps adults need to have control and make rules, this does not help children to feel that they have much control or choice and, when things go wrong, it reinforces the feeling that it must be their fault. After all, it could not be the fault of the adults, because the children see adults being right and all-powerful on a daily basis.

Just before contracting the herpes virus Angela had had the strong feeling, while having sex, that she would be caught and punished this time. She did not heed that warning. So afterwards, when it all happened and she was diagnosed with herpes, she hated herself for not listening to her own inner voice. She felt even more that it was all her own fault, and kept repeating: "If only I had listened!" It was hard for her to forgive herself. Angela was highly strung. She lacked self-confidence and had no real idea of where she was going or what she wanted to do in her life. In fact she always believed that her life and choices were limited because of her background and lack of academic qualifications.

Over time and very slowly, she began to deal with the shame and guilt. She began to be less fearful of her situation and more accepting. When I say fearful, I mean that Angela stopped feeling that she had been given a death sentence. She got more informed about her condition and started to have a small hope, which grew into a bigger hope. She began to believe that she could do something about her situation. She also became more accepting by realizing what had happened, and that although she could not turn back the clock, she could begin to take some control back in her life. However, as Angela kept reading and studying everything she could about her condition, she faltered and regressed. She once again lapsed into the belief that her situation could not be changed after all and that she was cursed forever.

Her healing process took the form of relaxation, meditation, researching and choosing an appropriate diet, and changing her lifestyle by choosing not to react in the same old ways to stressful situations. She was also a lot easier on herself. Each time she slipped, and reacted in those old ways, she would have an outbreak of the herpes. So in some way, frustrating as it was, she knew exactly when she was over doing things, worrying too much, being stressed and not taking care of herself. The outbreaks of herpes became her own personal barometer, a gauge of where she was in herself.

With time, Angela has gained much from this experience and continues to grow. Working on her career has been both challenging and rewarding in many ways. She has found belief in herself. And believing in herself remains her greatest goal and her greatest ally. Angela knows now that this is the way toward a total cure, and that a cure is indeed possible. Slowly, along her path, Angela has finally begun to love herself. She still does not have all of the answers, but she feels there is an end in sight and can hardly believe how very insecure and so out of touch with herself she had been before.

Anger of a child

When Darren came to see me, he appeared sullen and shy. I asked Darren to draw me a picture of his favorite things and talked to his mother for a while. He relaxed and seemed to enjoy using the different color pencils and crayons. His mother began her story. Darren, 11-years-old, was having lots of problems at school. He was angry and often lashed out physically at the other children. His schoolwork was poor. He had been diagnosed as ADD (Attention Deficit Disorder) and had been taking Ritalin for almost a year. His mother said that the medication seemed to keep him a little calmer, but he suffered side effects of nausea, irritability, poor appetite, and difficulty in focusing. Darren had been seeing a behavior psychologist for over a year. But the only conclusion reached was that he was angry.

I sat with Darren and his mother during our first session

and asked the child what he liked the most and the least in his life. I asked him about school, his friends, and his family. He loved his dog. He admitted that he was afraid of his anger, and thought it would end up getting him into trouble. He felt that he was a bad and out of control person.

Slowly more of Darren's story came out. His birth father had been a violent and abusive man. Darren's mother left taking her son with her. They moved to another state, and in time, she remarried a kind and gentle man who was a good husband and father to Darren and his new baby sister. Darren's birth father had legal rights to see his son, and had him visit for summer and Christmas holidays. Sadly, he often called his son and promised him visits that never happened. He also told his son that the break-up of the family was his mother's entire fault, that she had left him, told lies about him, and destroyed everything. Darren believed these things and, as a result, he often lashed out at his mother with rude words and clenched fists. She failed at these times to establish her own boundaries and accepted his bad behavior, believing somehow that it was her fault. Darren continued a regime of rudeness to his new stepfather, refusing to get along with him. The man was patient, but at a loss with what to do.

I gave Darren two rebirthings over a period of three months. The first one brought some improvement, but I felt a second one was needed. During the second session, Darren cried and expressed all of the pent up rage and anger he felt. A couple of weeks later, his mother called. Darren was no longer angry. He wrote the following short note to his stepfather: "I know you are not my real father, but you seem like a father to me."

As time went by, Darren finally came to realize that the break up of his mother and father was not his mother's fault. His father's broken promises and manipulative ways still affect him at times. But now, he has learned to express his feelings in positive ways. He writes things down, and goes outside to hit a punch bag if he gets angry, instead of hitting his mother and other children at school.

During the second rebirthing, I strongly suspected that sexual abuse had taken place with Darren in the past. His mother confirmed this later. She said that, at five-years-old, Darren had told her about "the bad things" his father had done to him. The case was investigated, but once the police and welfare services got involved and the father was questioned, Darren recounted back his statement and said that he had made it all up. The case was closed. No charges were filled. Sadly, this often happens, as abused children may have been told that, if they tell anyone about the abuse, the abuser will go to jail and they will never see that person again. Even when hurt, abused, and frightened, a child often does not want to accept that responsibility.

I still see Darren occasionally. He looks and acts like a different boy. For the first time this year, he told his mother that he does not want to visit his father for the summer break. He would not say why, but the mother let her son know that she would support his decision. She told me later that she was surprised and proud at how Darren had stood up to his father. Darren himself sees the future in a much brighter way now. He no longer sees his anger as a problem bigger than himself. He is almost off Ritalin medication. His mother confirmed that she knows that it's only a matter of time before Darren stops needing the medication all together. He is also doing well at school.

Buying time

Joan was a homemaker with three children and an organized and busy husband who was totally involved in running his own business. The family had enough money, but was always waiting for more. Joan had a very hectic schedule, always doing something with the children or the bookkeeping for her husband. She hardly ever had any time for herself and had no real hobbies. She admitted that it had been years since she really had even sat down and thought about whether there was anything missing from her life, anything that she wanted or needed for herself. Her husband expected her to be supportive and she was, seeing that as her main purpose in life. She was the supporter, the homemaker, and the one who nurtured others.

Joan was an attractive woman, with naturally blonde hair, and an open and pleasing face when she relaxed. She was slightly overweight, but it was barely noticeable. However, her weight bothered her. She did not feel good about herself and had a low self-esteem. Joan had regular cravings for sugar. She had been on thyroid medication for years, and also had allergies, especially during the spring. To have a red runny nose and runny eyes was almost a normal occurrence for her.

During one of our session, we focused on her allergies. She said she did not feel important or even really present a lot of the time. She felt that all the other mothers who picked up their children at school looked so well and seemed to have careers, to be very busy and important. She felt like an outsider. She also expressed the feeling that, although she was always busy and fulfilled with her role as mother and wife, she did not know who she was any more. Somewhere she had lost track of herself. She kept trying to be happy and pleased with what she had, but this did not work.

I used both rebirthing and regression sessions with Joan to clear and heal past emotional traumas. She began to realize how she used her allergies as a way of getting attention from everybody around her. She also used them as something to hold on to, something that others did not have control over, something that was hers alone, her problem, her situation. Joan almost felt she needed this, as she had to share most everything else in her life. Of course with children and a husband, she felt that it was good and right to share, and yet there was a little voice deep inside that felt she wanted something to be just hers, something that would make her feel individual and important.

Joan began changing her life. She started to take a few hours a week making quality time for herself. She began to write each day how she felt and what was happening in her thoughts and her world. This was an excellent way to let go. She realized that she did not need to continue having allergies just because she had always had them. She could say "enough" and bring change. Joan had a cabinet full of medications that had never brought any real cure from her allergies. She emptied the cabinet, throwing away the formulas one after another, swearing she would not take them or need them again.

One of Joan's biggest steps on her self-healing pathway was to begin a diet of positive news, keeping away from the allergy and pollen reports on TV and the negative news and headlines in the papers. Before, she had always worried about things like earthquakes or world war. After taking this action, her reality no longer consisted of negative news. In fact, if someone started to give her negative news, she would say kindly but firmly: "No, thank you, that is not part of my reality." It was not a case of turning a blind eye. Joan just came to the conclusion that she had a choice, and that she could live in her own positive reality and make it really be that way, day by day.

Six months later, Joan visited me again, this time looking radiant. She was eating a diet containing a lot of fresh fruits and vegetables. She confessed that she had almost beaten the sugar cravings and could hardly believe that she had so much more energy. She really felt great. She certainly looked well. Her nose was no longer red and runny. Her eyes were clear. In fact it was the first time I had ever seen her allergy-free. She confided that she had signed up to take a part-time healing course and had met some friendly, interesting people who liked her and seemed interested in her for who she really was. This was a very positive part of Joan's healing process. She realized that the people that she had felt alienated from in the past were not necessarily the people that she wanted to mix with anyway. She began to see that she was great just as she was, and always had been, and that there were people who could see and appreciate her for who she was. She did not need to compromise in order to fit in with anyone.

Now that Joan knows she has a tendency to put others first most of the time, she takes time for herself every few days to sit still and just be. She takes ten minutes to see how and where she really is, and to let go of all the tension that has built up and that she has been holding on to throughout the day. Joan not only no longer has allergies, she is also a much more confident and assertive person. At long last she feels fully present, no longer on automatic as if life was going on without her. She knows now that her health really is her own choice, as is her life.

I cannot emphasize enough how many people I see have some form of allergy such as sinus problems, head colds, sore throats, and runny eyes and nose. It's quite amazing. Each year, the number seems to increase. I notice that most of the time, allergies, as well as colds and flu, exist in people when they are buying time for themselves. They have not yet committed to clearing themselves, being well and moving on. A runny nose and eyes should be for them a constant reminder that it is time to look again and do something about their life. It is easy to prolong this situation without realizing it because of the huge amount of medication available to "control" the allergies. This merely postpones the time when sufferers realize they must look within, at themselves. Remember, allergies are not primarily a call for attention to the outside world and those around you, but rather a "wake up" call to yourself. It's time to stop leaving yourself on hold, but to give yourself now the attention that you need and deserve.

Chronic headache

Helen called me from out of state. She was concerned about her husband Jim because in all of their married life he seemed to always have a headache. This couple had been to doctors and specialists throughout their years together, but nothing had been found that could explain Jim's constant headache. It had got to the point where he could no longer work full time. Some days it was so bad that he could barely get up in the morning.

Not surprisingly, this was affecting their future plans. Helen was very successful in the sales and promotion fields and was ready to start out on her own with her own company. Jim was very excited about this too, because it meant that they could work together. He was great working with people and had an excellent record in public relations. But their plans at present were on hold, as Jim did not feel that he could function while he had this continuous headache.

They contacted me first by e-mail, then by phone, and decided to visit for the weekend. When I met them, I found that Helen was attractive, dynamic and had a pleasant personality, although she was perhaps a little tense and highly strung. Jim was much more laid back and relaxed but seemed rather introverted. I saw this couple both separately and together. Then we started to explore their lives, their relationship and their hopes and fears for the future. Helen went on to have a Rebirthing session as she was still carrying a lot of pain from her early childhood which she needed to release. She had grown up with a very dominating father and a passive mother, and had always felt the need to over-extend herself to gain the approval of others. Jim, who told me that he had had a headache even as a small child—in fact for as long as he could remember—chose the Regression session. This was exactly what he needed as he had a much more analytical nature and he needed to go back to past events and change the negatives into positives. He blamed himself for what he felt was poor judgment and decisions in the past.

During a session of healing where they were both present we realized that Jim had always been dreamy and creative but that this part of him had not been adequately expressed and he had also not felt confident and comfortable with himself. He rarely felt important or valuable. He often compared himself to others, and was also quite shy with groups of people and newcomers.

Jim, Helen and I worked together, each participating throughout the healing session. While we were working on Jim's forehead and crown chakra, we located what seemed to be an energy block. As it was released, so came the realization that Jim had held on to a headache all of his life as a focus point to remind himself that he was really here. He needed to feel solid and grounded. He had been using pain in this way for many years. He was excited about the future but unsure. This is where Helen participated. She reassured Jim that they would work things out together and that she was happy to slow down and do things in Jim's time. She reassured him also that deadlines were not necessary, and that their happiness and well being was paramount to her. Jim was relieved and truly accepted his wife's assurance. He was now released from the time pressure.

During the healing session and these realizations and affirmation, they both cried. Jim decided very seriously that he was not open to any more pain. The headache left shortly after, although it had been throbbing and very much present since they arrived.

Jim and Helen called me a few weeks later, happy to confirm that Jim had not had the headache since. Once or twice, when he began to have the thought of a headache, he sat still and relaxed until he felt in control again. After a lifetime, the headache was finally gone!

This is a small example of what is possible and you can begin to see that illness and imbalance do have identifiable causes. Each time we take another aspirin or another painkiller, we are keeping ourselves from dealing with the core issues, which will not leave by themselves.

This story also shows that you can work with partners and loved ones in your healing process, providing that you are both ready for change and each open to listening to what the other might need to express and reveal without blame or judgment.

Slowing down to catch up

John was classified as anorexic, and he also experienced anxiety attacks regularly. He was the father of three small children, one just a few months old. He was the primary earner in the family and had a well-paying position. But he hated his job. He just did not feel that he could find anything else that paid as well, given his limited skills. As time went by, he felt more and more stuck, but he continued to do his job well. He was a very efficient person and a methodical worker. But inside he felt like screaming. He wanted to take the fixed smile off his face and have someone notice how out of control he really was. This never happened, so he kept going.

As far as his family situation was concerned, they had had the three children very close together and his wife had not consulted him about the last one. As much as he loved all his family, he also felt completely stuck and controlled by them. So the anorexia and strict control over his intake of food gave him a way out, something to be in charge of in his out of control reality.

John knew that the anorexia had gone on for too long, that it was not a positive or healthy way for him to be, but he couldn't let it go either. He almost felt that if he let go of the anorexia at this point, there would be nothing left for him, nothing to hold on to at all. He did not have an active sex life with his wife or enjoy much intimacy with anyone. This was a problem which he found hard to talk about or to look at within himself. A lot of the time he felt cut off and dead from the inside. He described himself as feeling like a stone.

John had been getting serious headaches almost every day. He felt cold when it was warm. His words were: "I feel like ice is running through my veins." He often had a cold and had been having chest pains more frequently. It was time for John to slow down, to put everything on hold and put himself first before those minor health problems turned into even bigger ones. John knew this and finally agreed that it was a good idea to take some time off work. He took four whole days to stay in bed, just to rest, catch up on sleep, and to let the world go by. John told me later that he started using breathing exercises and techniques during those four days to finally deal with the anxiety. It helped him a great deal.

Another week passed. John had decided to take some further education classes and to start looking at other jobs for which he could become qualified. He realized that he really had needed four days to sit back and take stock of the situation, to put his life and his health into perspective. He understood that the anorexia was not going to go away by itself and that he needed to deal with it. He knew that in dealing with the anorexia and his issues of control, he needed to slow down again and dig deep into his present situation as well as the past. He needed to look at all of the things that had led up to this present point in his life. Because he felt he might need professional help working through the issues, he acquired a counselor. John learnt that anorexia is all about control. After taking another short break, he began to see things a lot more clearly, and he started to feel better than he had done in months. His constant daily headaches were rare now. His back didn't ache so often and his joints and muscles felt relieved.

John told me that during a spiritual bodywork and massage session, while the therapist was working on his shoulders and neck, he began to cry. He saw images of pain and sadness, distant images coming out of his shoulders from the past, memories of his childhood, the aloneness. He especially felt the aloneness that he had felt as a child and knew that was the part that had made him cry. He said that the crying was very healing for him during this session. It felt like a new beginning for him. Much of the pain was released during that massage session. John had had no idea of just how much memory and pain were held and stored in various parts of his body in those aching limbs.

John still had a long way to go, but he was now committed to himself and to being well and whole. He realized that he really could be happy. Later, he called me again and told me that life was beginning to make sense again, to really open up for him. He was on his own pathway of self-healing and awareness. His whole family became happier too.

Recently, John called and said he had started to put on weight and felt all right about it. He no longer needs the kind of control that the anorexia gave him. John feels that he still needs to work on issues of aloneness and intimacy, but he feels hopeful that he will reach the end of the process and find answers. Now that he is on his own healing pathway, he said that his wife feels that she can talk to him again, that she can now communicate her own issues and needs. She does not expect him to resolve everything for her, but she now feels that there is hope, that they can find closeness again in their once happy relationship.

John did almost all of his own self-healing work. All it took was his realization that he could, and that it was the time to get started.

Resignation—Giving up

Raj was an old man from India who had moved to

England in his mid-forties. He had had a stroke that affected the entire right side of his body, his face, part of his arm, his hand, and also his hips. He walked slowly with a limp, rarely going outside, but shuffling from room to room. His life was played out between the living room where he sat watching television and ate his meals, and the bedroom where he slept.

Raj watched everything closely and was aware of all that was going on around him. He didn't move around too much because of the stairs leading up to the apartment where he lived with his son, his daughter-in-law, and children. His wife had died just a year earlier. He did not want to live without her. She had been his "backbone" that had always kept him going. He had had the stroke days after she died; he did not really want to go on with life. He had been through rehabilitation in the hospital, and each day underwent physiotherapy there but with no lasting change in his condition.

His son engaged me in my capacity as a healer. During the initial session, I felt that I could work with Raj and help him. But from the very beginning, I let his son know that I did not believe that Raj wanted to live or change his condition.

I visited the family's home once a week, and gradually Raj started to improve. He could move around more easily with the help of a walking cane rather than needing to be constantly supported. His arm and hand were also becoming more flexible so that he could hold his own spoon for short periods of time to eat. He seemed pleased to see me during my visits. He liked to be the center of attention. I gave instructions that someone in the family should massage his arm, hands and feet each day. This task fell to the children. They took turns and he seemed to enjoy the ritual and the attention.

Raj's daughter-in-law already had two daughters. The old man wanted her to have a son. He held on to life only for this reason. He had no intention of really getting well. Nevertheless, he continued to be cooperative during my visits. It also helped his family to believe that he was making an effort after all. In reality, Raj liked to lie on the couch every day, doing nothing in particular. For him, there was no purpose or point to life. He only wanted to escape into his own world, his very own refuge that protected him from the real world where he was now alone. The aloneness he felt now that his wife was no longer with him was unbearable for him. He sat in front of the television for many hours each day, but did not appear to be really watching anything. I was another way for him simply to escape. His family members were busy people with their own lives, so it was convenient for them just to let him carry on escaping. I helped Raj to understand what he was doing and let him know that there was no point in my continuing to visit as a healer if he did not truly want to be well. I spoke to his son and told him how I felt. He reluctantly agreed with me and I stopped visiting.

Raj lived a few more months, long enough to hear news confirming that his daughter-in-law was pregnant with a boy. Soon after this, he was rushed to the hospital with pneumonia, an illness linked to the emotional heart center. He had never cleared this center or stopped grieving for his wife. I visited him in the hospital. He looked extremely peaceful and calm. He was pleased to see me. I felt a little sad for him as he lay there, a thin old man in a big hospital bed, green painted walls and nothing cheerful in the room to look at. But I knew Raj was at peace and ready to go soon. He welcomed death, and was certainly glad to leave this earth. I said goodbye.

Raj died two days after my visit. He had never really considered getting well or living without his beloved wife. She had been, in his mind, the other half of him. Raj's illness had been his refuge, a place to stay where people left him alone, allowed him to be and asked nothing of him. He used this refuge long enough to hear the news he was waiting for: the pregnancy of his daughter-in-law. Then he made ready to die. It did not matter to Raj if he died at home, or in the hospital. For him his life had already ended the day his wife had died. The stroke had been the effect of a massive shock to his nervous system and he had always been surprised, even perplexed, that he had survived. At last Raj had let go and gone to be, in his mind and his heart, back with his wife.

Means of escape—Refuge

Germaine and Pierre came from Europe to the United States on a two-week retreat vacation. They were in their seventies and had been married for over 45 years. Germaine had very bad arthritis in her hands. Her right hand had already been operated on, but the surgery had not helped and she was still in great pain. She also had diabetes and was a little overweight. Her hips and legs often ached. Her body was very stiff and uptight. Pierre was a small, thin and wiry man. He had had several eye surgeries and his sight continued to fail. He had a lot of panic, fear and anger about the thought of going blind. He felt useless, no longer needed or good for anything. He had hearing problems with both ears and also regular severe headaches. He was constantly agitated and stressed to the point of not being able to sit still for any length of time. When I first came in contact with Pierre, I was amazed at just how much tension he was holding in his body, especially his head. It would almost give me a headache just walking past him.

Germaine and Pierre brought with them a large bag of medication. During the first session, they both agreed that they did not wish to continue with all these pills. Germaine was in charge of their medication and the situation had become a little out of control. They had gotten to the point where neither of them was completely sure which tablet did exactly what, or even how long they had been taking them. My first directive was a total vegetarian diet with no meat or fish. I also asked them to cut down on fats and cheeses. I insisted that they drink as much room temperature water as they could each day. The climate in South-East Texas was a lot hotter than they were used to, so they needed the water to hydrate as well as to begin the process of clearing out their systems. It became quite a joke with Germaine, as one of us was always arriving with yet another glass of water for her to drink.

The other vital ingredient in their healing process was our "sit down and talk" sessions. They both had unresolved issues going back 40 years, things that they hadn't talked about with each other. These were issues that had been left unsaid and were buried deep down, and yet they shaped and dictated their present relationship. This affected not only how they communicated or didn't communicate with each other, but also how they viewed each other. There were often tense moments in these sessions. But issues were resolved and they both moved on. They each became quite quickly much more understanding, appreciative and friendly toward each other again, and they started to really talk.

Next, my husband introduced them to some gentle Tai Chi exercises. Pierre was especially happy with this. For the first time in years, he felt needed as he helped his wife to loosen up her body and master the basic moves. This was great for him, especially because he had been an amateur gymnast when he was young. It was obvious that he needed to feel useful. Now he had a chance, again, to shine and to excel. He came alive. He felt in control and needed.

The hand and wrist of Germaine was a stubborn area. It was without doubt an escape and a refuge for her. She empathized very much with the pain of other people she knew or came into contact with. Pain for her was normal and natural. Germaine had to learn to let go of pain, to take time for herself, and to face situations more calmly, reacting with less panic. This would indicate that she no longer needed the pain as a refuge for her suppressed intense emotions. It was good to watch Germaine as she continued to count each pain-free day. She had healed her hand.

This couple left needing only a small amount of medication, an amount that they would review when they arrived home. They were in high spirits with a whole new outlook on life. They also had a much more holistic understanding, and a positive approach to most things.

Pierre and Germaine still stay in touch with me, and two years later, they both are still doing Tai Chi. Their teacher proudly holds them up to others as an example and an inspiration because of the progress they have made and the commitment they express. He also applauds them because they have done all this in their seventies. After all, it is never too late to bring change and try something new.

Germaine did have one relapse when she returned home. I talked to her on the telephone and showed her again how to let her pain go and to stop empathizing with others. This worked and Germaine no longer has pain or arthritis in her hand. They both continue the vegetarian diet and feel well. Pierre is no longer afraid of losing his sight. The situation has now balanced itself, and is not getting worse. Furthermore, they do not expect it to. Whenever the couple does have even minor health problems, they sit down and discuss things, looking closely at what is really going on with them. Then they work through those deeper issues. Of course they still have issues from time to time, but they now both have more understanding and acceptance of their own healing pathway and of each other. They took one of my relaxation tapes with them and make time to use it and relax completely at least once each week. According to Pierre, this has been very helpful during their healing and staying well process.

Giving power to others and staying ill

Maria lived in Mexico. We had long distance telephone consultations and healing sessions. She had been confined to a wheelchair for four years when we first spoke. Before this, she had always been a very active person. She was diagnosed as having muscular dystrophy and was in a lot of pain most of the time. I initially recommended regular gentle massage sessions and the use of other nurturing techniques such as hot baths and reflexology. She agreed and later reported some improvement. The pain was no longer constant and she experienced greater flexibility in her muscles and limbs.

I knew quickly that Maria's situation had its roots in the past. It took a little time for this knowledge to be confirmed, but I was sure that her illness had started a while before it had physically manifested. This turned out to be the case. Maria was a wealthy woman. She had always had a good job and had enjoyed prominent social status. Working within the local government sector, she experienced power. She was also well-liked and respected and had the ear of men in important positions. She did a lot of good for others with that power and had a strong character, a keen sense of humor, and was quite comfortable speaking out about what she saw and felt when necessary.

Maria's husband had lost his job just before she started having the symptoms of muscular dystrophy. He had been in the same job for a number of years and had always been the main provider for the family up until that point. He was a very conscientious man in his work and seemed satisfied and happy with life in general. However, when he lost his job, his whole personality changed. He no longer wanted to go out or leave the house. He didn't want to look for another position, and he started to drink, which he had not done for many years. He also wanted to sleep late in the mornings and rarely had an appetite for food. He was irritable and moody.

Maria was often perplexed. She insisted, she begged, and she pleaded for him to change but nothing worked. He continued to mope around the house and had no interest in anything, not even his appearance that he once had taken great pride in. Maria was shocked and also a little afraid because he had always listened to her before. She had supported him in different ways and had felt that, although he was the man of the house and the highest earner, she really was the one who had the control over their lives. Now everything had changed, and she wanted the man she once knew back.

Soon after this, Maria began to get sick. Within six months, she could no longer work and was confined to a wheelchair. People around her were shocked at the dramatic change in her health. Luckily she had a good pension from her work to live on.

Then, life turned around again. Her husband's confidence began to grow. He started to look and feel well again. In fact the worse she got, the better he got. This might have seemed strange to an outsider, but Maria was preoccupied with her own problems and did not see the pattern at that time.

After a few healing sessions, Maria began to experience real improvement. She began to feel a lot better and started to have hope that she could be well again. She was very pleased. It was like a miracle. She felt her prayers were being answered. She became almost pain-free and her body was much more agile and flexible again. She was very happy. Then the process stopped. We hit a blank. She began to regress. Her health began once again to become worse. What was happening? There had to be a reason. And of course there was.

Just as Maria began to get well, her husband had started to become depressed, not caring about things so much, and letting himself go again. Somewhere deep inside of herself,

Maria realized that if she got worse, he would get better, and balance between them would be restored. And that is exactly what happened. Maria got worse and her husband started to care for himself again, to feel good about himself, and to open up to her. He was happy and back in control. He enjoyed taking care of her, and couldn't have been kinder. Neither of them was consciously aware at this point of what was happening between them.

During our next telephone session, I explained to Maria what was taking place. I made her understand that, somewhere in herself, she knew exactly what she was doing, that she was getting sick so her husband would be well. I showed her that she could choose to change this situation. But even knowing this, she decided not to change anything, not at that point anyway. Instead, she continued to be sick and to stay in her wheelchair. I stopped hearing from Maria once that point had been reached. She knew that I could help her and that she could help herself, but she had made her own choice, to stay sick for a while.

This is a classic case of a woman giving away her own power, her own health, and indeed her own wholeness. Maria gained a certain sense of security when her husband was happy, despite the personal pain that she accepted. Maria continued to be sick, and her husband felt secure in his being able to nurse her. He felt once more like the provider that he had once been. They had restored a kind of harmony between them. In a case such as this, it is generally only a matter of time before the sick person will reverse the situation and become well again. Then the relationship will need to be looked at again, and core issues addressed and resolved. There may even be a separation between the people involved.

This case is also a good example, not just of how we give away our own personal power, but also of how we sometimes allow the other person in a relationship to stay sick so that we can remain in control and feel needed. This scenario is played out in countless people's life. If we look carefully, we probably all know couples who act out this scenario to a lesser or greater degree.

Superstitions and illness

I have seen people, often belonging to ethnic groups and minorities, who are very superstitious. They accept, because of that deep superstition, all kinds of illnesses and diseases, especially wasting-type illnesses that cannot always be completely described or understood and yet are very real to the sufferer. Some of these people even die believing they have no choice. They just give up. In dealing with such people, I have learnt that they will not allow themselves to be helped unless they are really ready. Yet, they often spend vast amounts of money that they probably cannot afford, going to individuals who say they can help, but who actually perpetuate even more deeply the fear and superstition, and readily take their victim's money.

Ida, a middle-aged black woman, came to visit me. She had beautiful thick hair, deep eyes filled with pain, and wore a very sad expression on her face. She was overweight. She found it difficult to climb the stairs to my office, so we conducted our session downstairs. Ida had many different health concerns: diabetes, hypertension, heart problems, failing eyesight, very poor sleeping habits, cold sweats in the middle of the night, and panic attacks. Most of these problems had been with her for a long time. Ida looked as if she had suffered much in her life. She explained that she had one illness after the other. X-rays and tests often showed nothing. But still, Ida continued to have days where she could barely lift herself out of bed. She felt as if she was living with a huge, dark weight and shadow hanging over her. She kept going, but life was not joyful, only one long struggle after the other.

Ida worked hard in menial jobs and didn't get paid very well. She didn't complain. She felt that it was the best she could do and expect. She kept going to work as often as her health allowed. She felt that that lifestyle was her fate. Over the years Ida had spent a small fortune on potions, lotions, elixirs, and magical amulets. But nothing had helped with her poor health. She had visited many different psychics and faith healers over the years, believing and hoping each time that this next one would be the all-powerful who would save her from her darkened past, but to no avail. Nothing helped.

Ida began to tell her story. As she spoke, the past events unfolded for her as if they had happened only yesterday. Thirty years ago, Ida's husband had had an affair. He had left her and had stayed with his mistress for a short while. When the affair ended, the mistress decided to get revenge and paid for a curse against Ida and her husband. When Ida heard about the curse, her face broke out into deep red hives that lasted for two weeks. The scene was set. From then on, it was one thing after another, all through those past 30 years. Those were hard years for Ida who accepted her fate, sharing the details with no one except the practitioners she paid in the hope of being released from what she believed was a powerful and dreadful curse.

As I looked at Ida and got a picture of the mistress, and of those years in between, I realized that the cursing itself really had no actual power and no effect. But Ida's superstitious nature had caused her to believe in the curse. So she was constantly ill afterwards.

I saw this clearly and realized the truth of the situation without doubt. I also realized that it would be wise to let Ida relax and open up more, and to show her some things about herself and how life works. I knew that Ida would politely listen to reasoning and concepts, but that she needed solid proof then and there. These proofs came for her into the session, as they were needed. That afternoon, Ida came to understand that the curse had no real power and that she was in control. She realized she no longer needed to be ill or sick or stand in the shadows of life. She came to understand that life could and would be different and better from now on. She finally accepted this realization. She cried with relief.

Ida went through a healing and cleansing session, all of which she took most seriously, as indeed it was. Often, superstitious people need to have some type of cleansing ritual. We soaked her feet in hot water with sea salt and sandalwood oil. This helped her to feel safe, relaxed and open as I touched her shoulders, forehead and chest. It was as if the misery of the past years was rolling away. As I came upon different emotional traumas and disappointments locked into specific body parts, I told her about them and asked her to release them simply by closing her eyes and having the thought in her head: "I am letting go of everything I no longer need." I asked her to replace the deep red and gray colors that she perceived in her mind and that were for her colors of frustration and pain, with a shining white light. A lot of healing and release took place during the session, and Ida cried again. First it was tears of sorrow for all that she had been through, then tears of joy as she was released.

I met Ida's daughter a few months later. She told me Ida was a different woman. She just hadn't looked back. She seemed healthier. She had more excitement and fullness of life. She looked better, always smiled, and had lost some weight. She also had a keen interest in self-healing and staying well. Ida finally was free from her own superstition that had kept her enslaved and ill for so many years. I remembered how she had left our session that first day with so much relief that I felt satisfied and knew that she would move forward without looking back. And so she did.

Buying health

These events happened a number of years ago. Paul was

Jewish, in his mid-fifties and lived in London, England, when we first met. He came to me for a regression session. He had been in direct sales and marketing all of his life, and was recognized as a great businessman. He was a real cockney, an affectionate term for a Londoner, often an East Ender, who often has a strong accent. He had a lot of character, and was well liked wherever he went. Paul had a booming voice and when he spoke, people around him usually stopped to listen. He was an impressive figure, but at times, the little lost boy inside of him was very plain to see. It was hard for any woman not to fall in love with Paul, to mother him, and to take away all of that little lost boy's pain. Indeed Paul had no shortage of women in his life. But his heart was not open for romance and he was divorced and living alone when we met. He did have two grown children of whom he was extremely proud, but he was a little estranged from them. They didn't visit him as often as he would have liked, and that made him sad.

Paul was affluent. He had money to spend. He liked to enjoy life and he no longer needed to work hard to get what he wanted. He was established and lived in an exclusive part of town. The right address to him was everything. He smoked about a pack of cigarettes each day and although he rarely drank alcohol, when he did it was whiskey on the rocks. He was in quite good shape as far as physique was concerned. He did have a slight thickening around the waist and stomach, which he put down to the fact that he liked to eat well, often enjoying gourmet foods. Paul ate out most of the time, or had meals delivered to his residence from his favorite restaurants. He even had his favorites delivered from overseas.

Paul also had his own personal dietitian and nutritional consultant. His bathroom cabinets had rows upon rows of tablets, capsules, lotions and potions. There were vitamins, vitamin supplements, food supplements, and many kinds of rejuvenating products. Many of the herbs and potions were expensive items shipped specially to him from all around the world. Some of these products came from the Middle and Far East. I asked him what he took each day and it amounted to almost 50 different pieces, some tablets twice a day, others three times daily. His face did look fairly well. His skin was fresh, but not that well. He looked more like someone who had been pampered than someone who was in great health. He could be easily convinced to try any new products. He gave almost everything a chance and was considering, when I met him, trying the then-new animal hormone anti-aging treatment. He had his own personal Tai Chi and meditation master with whom he had worked for many years. And yet when I saw them work out together, I was surprised at what a novice Paul still appeared to be, and smiled at how boyishly he accepted praise.

Aging was definitely something that Paul was not going to accept. He had decided he was not going to get old. Paul had already had a face-lift, and had a tummy tuck scheduled within the following couple of months. Despite the weather in England, he always sported, even in the middle of winter, an excellent tanned body that was the result of a sun bed on which he spent many hours. His teeth were perfectly straight and perfectly white. He had spent a lot of time and money getting them exactly that way. Paul's knowledge of the New Age, self-help, self-improvement, and inspirational market was impressive. Two walls of his apartment were lined with a library of books and tapes collected over several years and devoted only to those subjects.

However, despite all of the care he lavished on himself, Paul did not find it easy to sleep. Much of the time he stayed up all night. He often appeared nervous, anxious and stressed, sometimes neurotic. In spite of the fortune he spent on his appearance and on educating himself, Paul had low self-confidence. He had been having coaching and elocution lessons for years, particularly trying to drop or disguise his very distinct cockney London accent. The accent made him feel inferior, and he would become defensive if anyone commented on it. Paul liked to mix in high circles and his money easily opened doors for him, and yet embarrassed as he was to admit it, he was ashamed of his humble working class roots.

Paul had a dry cough that never seemed to go away. He felt tired and without energy by early evening. He often had problems with his digestive system for which he tried all kinds of medications. Nothing worked. He spent a lot of the time trying to figure out why he was troubled so much with lower back pain. Nothing seemed to help, not even the special new orthopedic bed he had installed, although sleeping on the floor helped a little sometimes.

Paul also had poor concentration. He found it hard to listen to anyone else for more than five minutes at any one time. He was someone who might be accused of having selective hearing, although he tried to be open-minded.

Paul wrote poetry for pleasure. His poetry was mournful, deep, and very moving. It was inspired by a friend's wife who had died two years before we met. Paul had always felt that he had not done enough for that woman, and that her husband, once his good friend, was a selfish, uncaring man who had not deserved such a woman. He fantasized that he and that woman should have been together, and that she would have loved him beyond reason, beyond anything that had ever been thought, imagined or found between two people. When she died, he felt cheated, angry and sad. He was totally unable to let her go, or any of the events leading to her death. Yet he wanted to be happy. He wanted to be loved. Some days, he felt that it would be nice to fall in love again. He would catch himself with this thought, and then feel guilty thinking that he was being disloyal to this woman's memory and to the fantasy that he had created for both of them in his own mind.

Physically, despite all the help Paul was getting in his life and all the supplements he was taking, he still felt like a wreck.

Healing for Paul came slowly over time. We started with a consultation to put his situation into perspective. It took a lot for him to listen and to open up to the notion that there might just be another point of view besides his. He always spoke loudly, almost as if he were trying to block out everything except his own voice. During the course of a year, Paul went through two Rebirthing sessions to clear the deep emotional pain and anger he had been holding on to for so long, and other healing sessions. The healing and the Rebirthing sessions relieved the back pain. Paul was ecstatic because, on the physical level, he was pain-free at last.

We talked together a lot afterwards and Paul was able to listen more to different perspectives, and then to look deeper into his hurts and pains. It was Paul who did the expanding and opening; I acted as his sounding board. Past time Regression sessions revealed a horrific childhood. There had been abuse from an early age both physically and mentally from an outwardly loving and caring family. We worked together over a few more sessions to clear the trauma that had caused the shame within him, with its accompanying feelings of insecurity, low self-esteem, and low self-confidence that he had carried with him for so long.

Self-love came slowly for Paul, and we talked for many hours. In time, he realized that he did not need any master to teach him, slowly accepting that he could be the master himself. After that point was reached, his Tai Chi and Kung Fu sessions changed dramatically. He finally took and accepted control, to the surprise and delight of his teacher. Paul no longer needed rich foods or sweet and creamy substances in his stomach to fill his longing for love and calm. He began to find that calm and love were within himself. At last he could finally sit quietly alone. His waist diminished, the flabby stomach toned without the need for a tummy tuck. Paul began to look and feel great. He had more energy and vitality than he had had for years. He also had more time to listen to other people. His children began to visit him more regularly and they found peace again with him. Slowly he began to stop taking the vitamins and food supplements, realizing that his body just didn't need them. For the first time in years, Paul let his body tell him what it needed, rather than believing everything he read on labels and in the glossy health magazines that still poured into his mailbox. He became a vegetarian because he noticed that meat seemed to feel heavy in his stomach and took a long while to digest. He enjoyed the feeling of lightness that he now had.

One more thing still needed to be cleared: Love. It was time to let the past go. Together, Paul and I took a trip to see Steve, the husband of the woman who had died. Paul had once been close friends with Steve, before his bitterness kept them apart for some years. He had been blaming Steve for the death of Steve's wife, feeling she had not been cared for enough. They sat together and drank a beer that evening, slowly and quietly, neither speaking much. Steve, who was a musician, got out his guitar and strummed a few chords. Paul picked up a hand drum that was lying in the corner of the room and got a rhythm going. Finally, they got together again in music. Paul forgave. Later they began to talk about Steve's wife and all that she had meant to both of them. Then we left. Paul cried as we sped across the city in the taxicab. I had never seen him look so well. He body seemed to totally relax. The thin lines on his face disappeared and he looked as if he had shed a heavy load that he had been carrying for a long time.

We continued our sessions for a short while longer. Paul began to use the healing techniques that I showed him. He also developed more of his own healing techniques, using them instead of medicines. Now ironically he does not possess even an aspirin in the once full medicine cabinet. He no longer gets sick or has aches and pains that cannot be explained. He is well and balanced within himself and uses positive thoughts and affirmations to stay that way. Paul finally realized that he can take care of himself on an everyday basis, and that his health is not about how much money he spends. Life is a lot simpler for Paul these days. He feels finally at peace with the world and himself.

Healing cancer with self-belief

Ellen used to live in my neighborhood. She would come and visit from time to time and took part in various functions. She was originally from South Africa, and had two grown boys and a daughter. Ellen had lots of energy. In fact, she prided herself on having more energy than people 20 years younger than herself. She had a full-time job creating and supervising window dressings in a large department store, which was quite a demanding job. Ellen did not mind that because she could not sit still for ten minutes. She enjoyed having every moment of her day taken up being busy. She felt like a winner, important, busy. She had been this way for as long as she could remember. She lived in a huge house and could have had a cleaning person to help, but she preferred to do it all by herself. It would have seemed like a waste of money, she confided, although in reality money was not a problem for the family as her husband had an excellent, well-paying job.

Her husband, Tom, had been influenced by the English upper class in South Africa as a small boy. Now as an adult he was almost British in his reserve. He stood up very straight, and one might have thought he had been in the military. He had taken Ellen as a young woman away from the lonely and sometimes unhappy childhood that she had lived in a remote rural area with her parents and her younger brother. She had never had another boyfriend or looked at another man before or after their marriage. At first, she loved Tom's strength. Later she found it unbearably controlling, but could never imagine life without him. So she became submissive.

They moved to the United States when they were in their forties. Ellen loved to buy, and she loved to shop. If she was feeling down, a shopping trip would always give her a lift. She bought for herself, her grandchildren, her friends, her neighbors, everyone. For a few days after a trip, she felt happy and recharged. In fact, Ellen did not just go out to shop. She liked to shop via mail order and the shopping TV channels. She once invited me to her home and showed me her wardrobe. She had lines of outfits and shoes, everything perfectly labeled and packed away, but she lived in jeans and T-shirts, and she told me that she never really went anywhere in those other glamorous garments.

Ellen had always had a nervous cough in her throat and often felt a heavy weight on her chest. She liked to be liked. She did not wish to say an unkind or harsh word against anyone. Ellen was also quite a solitary person. She enjoyed her own company and could become claustrophobic in groups or crowds. She needed a Rebirthing session to start moving deep emotional blocks within herself. She cried during the session and allowed herself to really sob without holding back. She was surprised, never imagining that she could let go in that way.

Her life started to change. She was no longer prepared to be submissive. Four months later, Ellen went on Christmas break to Disneyland with her husband and all her children, and their wives, husbands and children. It was a disaster. One of her daughters-in-law was especially difficult to deal with at that time as she had problems in her marriage and could not get along with anyone. Ellen and the girl clashed badly. After all those years of being nice and patient with everyone, something in Ellen snapped. She had had enough. She told her son that he needed to sort out his problems with his wife, and that she could no longer deal with the bitterness between family members.

She returned home with a very bad headache and a cold, which quickly developed into pneumonia. Ellen had to stay in bed for two weeks. She was surprised, as she was not accustomed to being ill. When she recovered she was hardly the same person, being very quiet and withdrawn. It appeared to those around her as if she had a lot on her mind. She did not seem to want to do anything, or care much about anything during that time. She just wanted to sleep. Those who knew her wondered what could happen next.

Ellen called me and said she had to go to the hospital. She was diagnosed with Tuberculosis, which was another surprise as she had been vaccinated against TB as a child. The treatment for the Tuberculosis took several months. She came later to visit me for a healing session and indicated that a cancerous lump had been found in her breast, which would need to be removed. She looked fearful. At the same time, she was very focused and direct. She was ready to deal with the situation and do whatever was needed. She had total confidence that the cancer would be healed.

During the healing session, I helped Ellen to understand all of the repression that she had accepted throughout her life; how misused and mistreated she really felt by her husband, her children, and the various people she had worked for; and how she needed first of all to get in touch with and love herself. We talked about the fear that she was experiencing about the cancer, and how that fear was holding her back from realizing that she was the one in charge, that she could decide to bring change, that she could decide what happened next at this challenging time in her life. I showed her how to do specific regular breathing and healing exercises and color visualization to clear the affected part of her body. I kept going over the same points again and again. I told her that she was in control, that she could heal herself and that her healing would work. I explained to her that she would need to deal with and block out anything that made her think otherwise. She left that session feeling better and looking more relaxed, with a determined expression on her face.

Months later, Ellen called. She was calm, relieved and in a very positive mood. She had been for tests at the hospital and the lump was no longer there. She had the surrounding area tested and it was also clear. No one at the hospital could explain why it had gone, as she had not accepted any medication from the beginning. Ellen was quiet about the cure, but she completely believed in her own healing work, which had paid off.

Ellen still has some work to do. It does not always come easy for her to say exactly what she thinks and feels, but she is getting better. She shops a lot less these days and doesn't feel the need now to read endless healing, inspirational and self-help books. She now has a much more positive and assured knowledge that she is the one who can really heal, because she has already proved it to herself. Ellen is not the kind of person to share her testimony of self-healing with anyone, but those close to her know what happened and now listen more carefully to her opinions and beliefs. In fact, in her own quiet yet determined way, she continues to change and inspire many people around her to look again at their own lives and health issues.

Will power and faith alone are not always enough

Paula called me about a very personal situation that had been affecting her for over 10 years. Since the birth of her second child, her colon no longer functioned properly. She had to use laxatives and enemas just to function and dispose of bodily waste. After years of feeling drained, tired, physically uncomfortable and mentally exhausted, she found a medical specialist who understood her condition. He had researched and operated on other women with her symptoms. Paula talked to this doctor at some length and, as a final option, was reluctantly considering surgery for her situation. She liked and trusted the doctor, but surgery was for her the very last choice.

Paula, who lived in the United States, heard about a world famous healer who lived in Austria. She had to wait quite a while to see this man. Finally the day came. She flew over and stayed for the first night in the best hotel that she could find. She wanted to feel rested and ready. Having waited for months for the meeting she had built up her belief in this healer, and she felt that she was finally going to be healed. She felt that she had been led to him, that finally her nightmare would be over, and that she would be able to get on with her life. Her daughter was an unmarried mother and needed her help, and her own career as an artist and writer had been on hold for too long.

On the morning of her first meeting with the healer and psychic surgeon, she wrapped her thick coat firmly around her body against the cold European winter chill. She felt extremely positive and relieved, as she had already conferred with him on the telephone and he was both positive and optimistic, sure that he could help her.

Paula stayed for over a week at the clinic and had healing sessions each day with the healer. He went into a trance every time he conducted a session and allowed a spirit doctor to use his body and work through him. During the final session, the spirit doctor told Paula that she needed to relax, to change her lifestyle and diet, that she was a beautiful person, and that she could go home now as everything was over and she was finally healed. Paula was elated. She packed her suitcase and took an earlier flight than planned. She just wanted to get home. It had been an emotionally charged week, and a nightmare of many years was finally over, she thought.

Back home she waited. But nothing had in fact changed. Her situation was still the same. She was not cured and not cleared. Paula was quite devastated. After all those months of waiting and believing, not to mention the money she had spent on the trip, she was incredulous and confused. How could he have been so sure she was healed?

The lesson here is that faith alone, or simply wanting things to change, may not be enough. And the healer, no matter how much he believes in himself and his work, may need to look deeper into a client's situations and problems, and see what is really going on. Certainly, this healer meant well and did his healing work. Perhaps he was too busy to give this woman the individual help that her case required. Without a doubt, he did not look deeply enough at his results or even expected results. Perhaps he even imagined that as he was a great healer, Paula would allow herself to heal because of her belief in him. In this case, it simply did not work.

When self-healing or any kind of healing does not work for you, simply understand that you have not yet got to the root cause. But with persistence you can and will.

The doctor/guru superpower belief system

Alex was a working psychic and believed in the power of healing. He was in his late fifties when he got sad and heart-sick. He started to cough a lot, put on weight, and withdrew within himself. He also started to express a lot of anger to those around him and closest to him. This made everyone feel anxious and sad, because he had always been a very kind and balanced person.

Alex came from a generation of people who worshiped the family doctors almost as if they were gods. The doctor always knew best. No one in those times would dream of arguing with a doctor or presumed for a moment to know better than the expert. During that time, in the 1940's and 1950's, penicillin and antibiotics were miracle tablets. They cured everything. This added to the wonder, esteem and awe in which doctors were held. Although Alex could captivate audiences by saying things such as "I am everything," and genuinely knew and believed this about himself, when it came to his own bouts of illness, it was entirely another matter. He had such a built-in indoctrination about doctors knowing best, he could not get on with the process of healing himself. He continued to help others with their own problems, but kept visiting the doctors for medication without questioning their recommendations.

Alex was married to a woman who felt insecure a lot of the time. She believed that her husband was very attractive to other women, and she felt very lucky to be with him. Her insecurity came from an unhappy childhood and two previous abusive marriages. Alex, who was one of twelve children of a poor family, had never got full attention in his early years, and he was feeding his wife's beliefs and insecurities so that she would always be paying full attention to him. This kept her in control. Meanwhile, she was happy, subconsciously, that he was sick, because she felt she could then love, nurture and control Alex and the situation. There was no way in which he would run off and leave her while he was ill, which had always been her greatest fear. So she nursed him, fed him with sweet cakes, puddings and other not especially healthy foods, and talked in hushed tones when he took naps during the day. She became very protective of him and his poor health, letting family members and friends know how ill he was, and asking them not to let him get upset or angry in any way as this would worsen his condition.

The result was that Alex got very old very fast. He put on weight and became more and more convinced over the next 18 months that he was very ill. His doctors tried one antibiotic and steroid after another to help fight infections and to clear his lungs, which, they assured Alex, had been very damaged. At one point he was diagnosed as having lung disease.

Alex faithfully continued taking his medications over a period of two years, never seeming to get any better. Despite flu shots each winter, he still had bouts of flu and various other chest problems. Alex also got angrier with himself, his wife and everyone else around him. If he upset anyone, they would swallow their hurt, because, after all, he was ill. So Alex lost touch with other peoples' boundaries. Expressing anger, hurting himself and others became normal and almost acceptable for him.

Finally his doctor admitted that he had been misdiagnosed. Alex didn't really have lung disease after all. Although his lungs had not gotten any better, they hadn't gotten any worse either over the two-year period. They were at a standstill. The doctor then recommended another specialist, who later said that he could not really say what was wrong with Alex either. The doctors however were willing to try new medications.

Alex called me at this time. He seemed almost amused at being used as a guinea pig. I asked him how long he expected to be on the various medications. He said: "Forever. All of my life, I suppose." I asked him later, during another conversation, what he thought of his situation after all that had happened. He admitted that he did not have much faith now in professional opinions and it would probably just be a matter of time before he stopped taking all the medications and started to heal himself. He knew very well that he could heal himself, and that his health condition was up to him. He had just gone a long way away from himself, giving a lot of his power to others.

Alex had finally arrived back with himself and his own

self-belief, but not until he had let go of the notion that others should and did know better than him about his health. As an intelligent man, Alex later was bemused at how his own upbringing had led him to have such a strong doctor/guru superpower concept, while at the same time he had always had such an equally strong belief in himself. But still, it had happened.

Fear and acceptance

Sophie was a petite, attractive woman. She had a lovely smile that made her whole face come to life. When she came to visit me the first time, she brought many answered questions with her. I knew right away that she had realized that it was time to change her life, to break down the walls around her that she had accepted, and to get back to the amazing person she remembered being. It was never a matter of her wanting my help. Rather Sophie knew that I would understand who she was beyond any of the circumstances in which she found herself, and be able to see where she was within herself at that moment in time. In many ways, Sophie needed to be recognized.

By looking in her eyes and giving her my full attention, I sensed immediately that her forehead area was blocked with a build up of uncleared thoughts. Sophie was holding on to a lot of information, and also self-doubt, mainly because a lot was going on in her life and with her family, and she had not made time for herself to process and let go. She had put the letting go process on hold for too long, but was ready now to start.

One of the reasons she knew that it was time was because of the constant headaches she was getting. She did not like taking painkillers, but there did not seem time to do anything else. Sophie drank a lot of carbonated drinks, containing large amounts of sugar, which was also not helping the forehead area, or her ability to focus, and made her feel that she could not think or see straight.

Sophie has been taking a well-known anti-depressant for over a year when we met. This calmed her down, but also made her feel even more blocked. She told me that it kept her calm and took away the need for the explosive outbursts to which she had been prone. Her outbursts were actually the expression of her frustration and anger with all that was not right in her life. But at that time she did not feel she had the right to express herself and upset the balance of her family and others around her. Instead, she took the anti-depressant as a form of suppression. It had worked, but Sophie was tired of not feeling good and she was concerned about the effect the medication was having on her body.

Sophie was also taking medication for a thyroid imbalance which had been diagnosed almost two years earlier. From the beginning, she had accepted the thyroid imbalance. It was a condition already known in her family. Her mother had it, and her sister-in-law and a few of her friends had it too. It seemed to Sophie that it was something that women got at a certain age. So reaching that age she had accepted it as her own and had fit in with everyone else.

Most of the people around her had something wrong with them. Being unwell and on medication was a normal part of everyday life and conversation for her. Sophie did not want at that time to draw attention to herself by being well, happy and free. Instead, like a special undercover agent, she preferred to remain unnoticed. She fit in with the thyroid problem, the headaches and the general feeling of being unwell, just like everyone else.

But it was not just that simple. On the one hand, Sophie had a sure knowledge that she was just "fitting in" and did not in fact need to be unwell. On the other hand, she half believed in a fearful way that the thyroid problem was real, that it was inherited, and that she was stuck with it. Sophie was an intelligent woman, and she decided that it was time for change. She began to step back and look at her life. She saw that, at that time, she felt locked in an unhappy and mainly unfulfilling marriage to a man who had a high-profile job, but who was constantly stressed. He acted most of the time in a very authoritarian and rigid manner, and was not the loving husband and father to their two young daughters that she wanted him to be. It was a second marriage for them both, and they each had grown-up children at college who also were a source of stress as there were problems with their grades.

Sophie had reached a breaking point. Something had to change. No matter how hard she tried, she felt as if everything that went wrong was somehow her fault. Her husband was constantly telling her that she was the one with the problems, so she had reached the point of believing that it was the case.

Just before our meeting, Sophie had started weekly counseling sessions. She started to talk through her problems, her thoughts, her feelings and fears. She had begun to see that it might not be all her fault after all. This helped her to feel more empowered, and more hopeful that change was possible. Simply having someone outside of her situation, who would listen while she unraveled her thoughts and emotions, was her first step on her own self-healing path. She started to gain perspective.

Sophie and I worked together on and off for a few months. She found herself being more assertive and expressing her feelings. She discovered different ways to deal with stress including a regular massage and taking time out for herself to walk or read. Some days, instead of being completely busy, she took a day off and spent time in ways that made her feel good. She stopped accepting that everything was her fault, and that she had to be unwell to fit in with everyone else. Sophie especially liked and followed the self-healing and clearing exercises, and made them a part of her life when necessary.

Sophie became well and happy again. Those around her noticed it and asked for her secret. She gradually got off the depression medication, as she had learned how to express and deal with core issues and no longer felt depressed or out of control. During her last visit to her doctor, she was delighted when he pronounced her clear of her thyroid problem. He could no longer find any sign of imbalance. So she stopped taking her thyroid medication too.

Sophie had over time a Rebirthing session and three Regressions to help her heal her past. She also had a mediumship session and cried when she made contact with a dear friend who had passed on some years before. This session took away her previous fear of death and helped her to open up to many new ideas. She has now moved away and lives with her family in a northern state. She continues to develop her awareness and uses her own healing abilities to help herself and her family. Sophie found it easier and easier as time went by to find her own answers to her questions. She simply sat still, let the answers come, and then followed them through. The last time we spoke, she told me how amazing life is and how well it works for her these days.

Chapter 11

Medicine, Self-Healing and the Future

ॐ

Projections and expectations of future medicine

Where is medicine heading in the twenty-first century? There are many positive expectations and projections. The front cover of Popular Science, October 1999, depicts a "futurist human being" with the heading: "Body of the Future: New drugs, high tech repairs and revolutionary transplants conquer disease and extend our lives." In an article titled "Bodies by design," Frank Vizard states that transplants, which were once used strictly as life-saving procedures, are now being performed to improve patients' quality of life. For example, two people have recently had a hand transplant, one in Australia and the other in the United States. Both operations were a success, but each patient will face a lifetime of taking drugs.

Because of the low availability of human organs, the feasibility of using pig organs is being researched. A breed of genetically engineered pigs will produce human protein, which will be able to hide the pig organ from the human immune system and so avoid rejection of the transplanted organ. Scientists estimate that they will be able to test pig organs on humans in two to five years.

Another article in this magazine notes that, while electronic implants have already been used with remarkable success for restoring hearing, this new technology offers astonishing promise for some people who are blind and cannot be treated today in any other way.

Parkinson's disease is also in the news. Apparently, scientists have been studying an experimental therapy that implants fetal pig cells in the human brain. The magazine includes articles about the latest results of Gene Therapy and new artificial body parts, such as a battery powered hand that offers patients the use of all five fingers making seemingly impossible tasks, like playing piano, a reality. This artificial hand is planned to be available to the public next year. Artificial eyes, ears and noses that are virtually indistinguishable from the genuine human parts are also now available.

Over the past few months, there has been a lot of other information reported in widely available magazines on the expectations and projections of future medical solutions. Jocie Glavsiosz, in an article titled "Spare Parts: Bioengineers foresee a time when you can grow your own organs," (Discover, June, 1999) states: "The human body is an infuriating mix of fallibility and intolerance. When vital organs wear out and break down, the immune system stubbornly fights and attempts to replace them. More than 60,000 Americans are waiting for transplants. Those lucky enough to receive a donor organ, will face a daunting fight for survival." The author adds that in years to come patients may overcome problems of organ rejection by getting spare body parts made from their own cells. Robert Langer, of the Massachusetts Institute of Technology, and other bioengineers, envision a time when all replaceable organs will be grown in the lab. The article gives examples of what this could mean:

A steady supply of arteries may transform heart bypass surgery; artificial nerves could one day carry electrical signals between severed neurons; a liver nurtured in the lab would benefit the 3,000 Americans waiting for a transplant; a bioengineered pancreas, lab ripened and insulin producing may ease a diabetics' symptoms; fresh intestines could replace tissues exercised after colon cancer, bioengineered bladders may soon provide relief from disease; a clear new cornea constructed with cells removed from a healthy eye could replace one clouded by disease; replacement skin already available heals leg ulcers and severe burns; fresh, healthy breast tissue could fill the space left by mastectomy; newly grown bones and joints may some day be built from specially cultured cells in combination with body compatible polymers, a lab grown kidney would clean the blood as well as protect the body from infection; lab-created cartilage could repair damaged knees and other body parts.

In another article titled "Immortal Cells," written by Shanti Menon and published in the same magazine, the author reports that "the clusters of human skin cells basking in a sterile incubator with alarms poised to go off if the level of carbon dioxide drops or the temperature wavers from 98.6 degrees appears to be blessed with eternal youth. Under normal circumstances, skin cells divide about 50 to 70 times and quickly wither and stop dividing."

The article goes on to say that after two years in a laboratory at Geron, a Menlo Park, California Biotech Company, these genetically altered cells are approaching 400 divisions and still show no signs of aging. They just keep multiplying. Until now, endlessly multiplying cells only indicated cancer, but biochemist Cal Harley and cell biologist Jerry Shay, who have the same type of lab set up at the University of Texas Southwestern Medical Center in Dallas, say that the remarkably youthful skin cells remain cancer-free. Harley and Shay hope that their success in prolonging the life span of these individual cells in the lab could eventually pave the way for more people to lead healthy and productive lives up to the age of 120 years.

Each and every day breakthroughs are envisioned and made within science, medicine and technology. Humankind moves on and it is exciting to realize that what might have been seen in previous years as miracles are now becoming possible. It is interesting, as we ponder these great breakthroughs, to question what will become more widespread in the future. Will it be healing through technology, or through further awareness within individuals that we do not need to be ill in the first place, and that we can heal ourselves even in what would previously have been considered dire circumstances?

Building a brighter and better future

The following anecdote is a small example of the way things are in our society today. I use it to show how difficult it seems to trust, to let go, even to accept spontaneity in our lives. Yet, at the same time, it also only takes a moment to break through each and every predefined barrier in existence.

My 14-year-old daughter and I were recently playing in the swimming pool of a hotel complex. A grandfather and his young granddaughter were also in the pool. The little girl might have been five years old. The grandmother sat outside the pool watching my daughter and I as we played catch with a beach ball. In a corner of the pool, a little boy was playing all alone. He was about seven years old. His mother lay on a sun lounger watching him swim. Our ball went in his direction a couple of times and he threw it back to us. He was enjoying doing that so I started to include him in our game.

The reactions from people around were amazing to me. My daughter graciously went along with including the small boy in our game for a while, but she was also clearly a little jealous at the attention he was now getting which was no longer completely focused on her. The mother of the child did not acknowledge with either a look, a smile or a nod that we were playing together with her son. Instead, she kept her eyes rigidly fixed and locked on her small son. The two grandparents were clearly nervous and exchanged anxious looks between them. They remained tight-lipped and tight-faced and seemingly over-protective of their small granddaughter, calling her away as she tried to join our game once or twice too. The little boy remained oblivious to all of this and enjoyed the game anyway.

Ignoring these other reactions, after a while I gave the ball to the little boy and got out of the pool. The boy's mother continued to ignore everything that was going on around her, only keeping her gaze fixed on her son. The grandparents of the little girl insisted on hurrying their granddaughter out of the pool even though they had not long arrived and she was clearly enjoying herself. My daughter retreated into her own world, practicing her underwater swimming techniques. So everyone, including myself, cut off from the scene and retreated into their own space.

I can understand people being cautious with children, but this was in broad daylight, and in an exclusive hotel. The little boy was not physically approached or touched in any way. He was just included in a game that was already going on which he clearly wanted to play in. I was not looking strange, or weird or behaving in any unusual way, simply being a mother playing with a beach ball in a pool with my daughter.

I can speculate on what might have been going through each one of these people's minds. But for me, it shows where we are with ourselves as adults, and how very suspicious we are of anything even slightly out of the ordinary. More than that, it makes me realize how difficult it is for people to reach out, to accept or to include anyone or anything that is outside their immediate controlled reality. Yet there is so much more to explore, to experience, to have and to be if only we look a little further and open ourselves a little more to life and reality.

If we look at our reality, we will realize that many of us do not know our next-door neighbor, or have never spoken to the people we pass each day as we go to work. We lock our doors and we live in fear, thankful that the horrors going on outside are not happening to us personally. I do not usually watch television or read newspapers. When I do, I can easily see that the media is a powerful tool and often focuses on the negative issues a lot of the time. I understand that people who accept the negative news constantly bombarded at them receive strong negative images about our world and reality. It is easy then to see why so many people are living in fear. But remember, all that you are accepting is by choice. Each one of us can say today that negative news is no longer part of our reality. So, don't just sit back waiting for reality to change and dreaming, hoping, and wishing that it will change one day. Instead we can individually participate to make the changes happen now. It is easy to blame governments and social systems that do not seem to work for everyone. But let's not forget that we created those systems in the first place. They are not a machine out of control despite what you may have read. Systems and governments are made up of people who are fundamentally the same as us. We, each one of us, have a right to say how we feel and to bring change to our world.

What does it take for us to care enough? Personally, I

don't believe that it will take very much. I don't believe that we need disasters and wars or any other traumatic events to bring the changes that are needed for mankind to move on. What is necessary is that each person sits down, thinks, and makes a decision that reality as it is today is not good enough, that we can all expect and have so much more. Then each person must decide to accept no more compromise, but expect and accept the best.

Breaking routine and patterns

We accept routine in our lives mainly because that is how our society is structured. Although we may strike out against this structure sometimes, even debate it, we do little to change. If we want to enjoy the basics and also the benefits of the society in which we live, routine plays a large part in our daily lives. For example, we get up at a certain time. We go to work when we have to. We send our children to school at an appointed time. There are options, of course, such as home schooling for children, or having your own business. But these options still have routines to follow, even though they may be more relaxed. They are your own routines rather than someone else's. There are people who do remain awake, aware and conscious, living within routines, but for the most part, people become blasé, apathetic, dull, jaded, and burnt out when living in routines over long periods of time.

Often people who have found awareness or who have looked at life in depth have done so because they took time out and let go of routine in their lives. Each and every person can find his or her own way of doing this, be it taking a week off, a year off, or a lifetime away from routine. Even just driving or walking a different way to work breaks routine and allows room for change to happen. Perhaps making a decision not to do what you usually do every Christmas or every Thursday night could be a start and make a real difference.

The options and changes that we can each make are endless, but see for yourself how changing and breaking routines can bring positive change in your life and allow you room to breathe. Allow yourself today greater awareness and perspective in the everyday by breaking routine and patterns. Expect the unexpected, the miraculous and the wonderful to happen. Open yourself to receiving all that you feel is missing in your life. Above all, give yourself room for change to occur and the space to perceive life, yourself and others in previously unthought of and unexpected ways. After all, life and circumstances may not be what is limiting you at all. "You" could be the very one that is limiting your own life experience by simply not breaking out now and again from patterns and routines.

A glimpse into the future

Just exactly where are we heading with self-healing? What is the future of medicine, wholeness and wellness as we move into the third millennium? I conclude this book by taking a look into the future. To do this, I used Progression as an aid to help me relax to the point of moving forward in time and viewing future events. Individuals can use Progression Therapy to go forward days, months or years ahead in time to find answers to their own questions. I have been successfully working with progression for a number of years. I have even taken skeptics ahead in time on television and reporters for magazines, and have documented positive feedback and results. We can all use Progression quite naturally, and I will write about this technique more in details in a future book. Some of the things that I saw when I progressed fifty years into the future may in part help to explain why self-healing is so important for us now, why we need to become committed, for self-healing is already within us, a part of our present reality and an even bigger part of our future.

I choose a peaceful sunny place at the beach. It was early

morning, and few people were out. The sun was just rising and the waves were gently lapping the shoreline. I stretched out comfortably on the sand and began to progress by breathing deeply and casting my mind ahead to a fixed point. The year was 2050. Moments passed. My focus sharpened. After arriving at this timespace, I observed how life and reality was within the self-healing and medical fields. Then I moved backwards in time and space to more recent times to see how future developments had been reached.

I saw that disease and illness in 2050 are mainly seen as a reality of the past, and that the majority of people worldwide are healthy. They do not get ill, but stay well and in balance, more so than ever before. People have literally outgrown disease, simply because more and more people have become aware of the choice that they have to be well, rather than ill. Mankind has come of age. There are exceptions but wellness is now a reality for the majority rather than the minority.

Science and medicine work closely together at this time. Doctors and scientists working together come under the same title, they are technicians. They continue to learn about and to understand the human body and its mechanics. To be ill in 2050 is viewed more as a psychological imbalance and disturbance. There are extremes however, because in this time, when people do get ill, it is with either very simple maladies or very complex ones. There is rarely anything in between. The diseases we currently know such as cancer, Parkinson's disease, heart attack and strokes were eradicated between 2030 and 2040.

These technicians and individual healers understand the brain and how it functions much more than in our present time. Healing is centered around the head, the spinal cord, the spine, the brain stem and the nervous system. These points prove to be important keys to unlocking the knowledge of the human body. Individuals will discover and develop knowledge of how touch and manipulation of these parts work. Healing also takes place with the understanding and the readjusting of vibrations and vibratory patterns. Doses of colors and vibrations are administered to specific sections of the head. The mystery of the skull is now understood and makes sense. Interestingly, I hear that at this time, many contemporary crystal skulls are coming out of China. Many are being now carved in great details, including the brain stem.

I see that the answer to imbalance in this time is primarily vibration, and both complex and simple readjustments are made by individuals and technicians. Medication is now rarely given or used. When it is given, it is powerful and complex, and is taken over a short period of time, generally no more than three to four days. Medication is only administered over a short period of time because technicians now understand what takes places during those first few days of healing and recovery.

There are just a few different types of medication available and used in the year 2050. The primary function of the medication is to amplify the body's own natural healing process. The beginning of this breakthrough will be discovered twelve years from now, around the year 2012. A researcher living in Poland makes an important discovery in his studies of the human body's actions and reactions to disease. An important corner is turned at that point. India also greatly contributes with breakthroughs in understanding human vibratory patterns. The United States plays an important part by giving financial support and resources worldwide to develop programs in these different fields.

Thirty-five years from now, much of the research and experimentation that is new today is complete and conclusions have been reached. A lot of money has been spent, but most of the data collected is inconclusive and later abandoned. Within this thirty-five year period, genetic engineering will lose support from the public and will not achieve all that its advocates initially hoped for. It will be realized that the formulas for pain-free and disease-free humankind are not going to be found in that area after all.

Imagine a solid tree with many branches; we can call it the tree of life. It is as if medicine needs to follow and investigate all of its branches to see where each is heading and what can be done, before resources and research finally comes back to the original trunk, and life itself: the spine, the spinal chord, the brain and the brain stem.

In the year 2050 societies and individuals will be aware enough and strong enough as a whole not to accept imbalance and illness within themselves. A large positive change will take place. This is also a big part of why so many people are now investigating and discovering self-healing. It is also why it is so important for individuals to take this path today, because each participating individual will be a part of and facilitate the shift for mankind into an age of wellness and wholeness.

As we look ahead, then, and see where self-healing is going, we realize that we are opening up pathways within ourselves now and for future mankind to live in a pain-free, balanced, whole and healthy society. At present the tabloids and mass media campaigns would have us believe otherwise. We are lead to believe that we need medication, natural or not, and all other kinds of help, to a degree almost never reached before, just to stay alive and cope with our present and future living conditions. We are told that we are coming into an age where many new diseases are to be expected. This is good news for the pharmaceutical and natural remedies industry. But it does not have to be our reality.

Remember, you can have a life and a world with no more illness and no more pain. By deciding for yourself, you help decide for everyone else. You decide also for the future. For we are each linked one to the other, and each one of us is a facet of a greater whole, as well as, at the same moment, individual and complete. As we accept self-healing into our lives, we celebrate the greatness and joyfulness of our own being.

Enjoy and benefit from self-healing, and remember, I am amazing and **you are amazing too.** Now is the time to believe in yourself and let the magic be!

Index

✍

Visit Petrene's Internet site at http://petrene.com

- Find out about upcoming events;

- Listen to extracts of talk shows;

- Read articles on self-healing and self-awareness;

- Help others by sharing your own self-healing experiences;

- Meet others with similar interests and participate in Petrene's Chat room, Forums on self-healing, awareness and ESP, and "Ask Petrene" section;

- Subscribe to OPENINGS, our exciting and stimulating free electronic newsletter;

- Take time for yourself and experience the exclusive free Color, Focus and Meditation Rooms.

"The site is packed with answers and inspiration, and offers you a chance to meet with others and participate in experiences that will change your life in countless positive ways. Don't forget to say "Hi" by signing the guest book. It's always great to hear from you! And do take advantage of the option to schedule your own chat; I will be personally participating in chats whenever possible. I am really excited about the site and look forward to your discovery and enjoyment too. After all, this site is about you and designed just for you."
—Petrene Soames

Fast Order Form

Fax: Fax this form to (281) 292-1650

Telephone: Call Toll Free (888) 263-9637 with your credit card ready.

E-Mail: Send information below to orders@petrene.com

Internet: Go to http://petrene.com/order.html [secured order].

Postal Order: Send this form to FleetStreet Publications, Petrene Soames, Box 130416, Spring, TX 77393-0416.

Please send me ❏ one copy ❏ _____copies of *The Essence of Self-Healing* ($14.95 each).

Please send more information on:
❏ Other books ❏ Seminars ❏ Consulting

Name: _____

Address:_____

City: _____State: _____Zip: _____-_____

Telephone:_____

E-Mail Address:_____

Sales Tax: Please add 6.25% for books shipped to Texas addresses.

Shipping: Add (after taxes if applicable) $4.00 for the first book, and $2.00 for each additional book.

International: Add $9.00 for first book, and $5.00 for each additional book.

Payment: ❏ Check ❏ Money Order
    ❏ Credit Card: ❏ Visa ❏ Master Card ❏ AMEX ❏ Discover

Card Number: _____

Name on Card: _____Exp. Date: ___ / ___

Signature: _____